The Foundation to

Promote Personal Responsibility

A collection of essays on fiscally conservative thoughts

Includes **The 2020 Initiative –**

A nonpartisan solution to the federal government's
growing debt problem

[$20 Trillion and rising, with no end in sight]

To our families and fellow countrymen
and to future generations

Freedom is never more than one generation away from extinction. We didn't
pass it to our children in the bloodstream. It must be fought for, protected,
and handed on for them to do the same. - Ronald Reagan

For information about special discounts for bulk purchases of the paperback
version of The 2020 Initiative and The Foundation to Promote Personal
Responsibility, please send an email to info@f2ppr.org

Special Thanks to –

George Washington, Thomas Jefferson, James Madison, Alexander Hamilton,
Abraham Lincoln, Alexis de Tocqueville, Ayn Rand, Ronald Reagan, Antonin
Scalia, Oliver DeMille, The Heritage Foundation, The Cato Institute, and
Hillsdale College

The 2020 Initiative
ISBN 978-0-9994432-1-7   (paperback)
ISBN 978-0-9994432-3-1   (ebook)

The Foundation to Promote Personal Responsibility
ISBN 978-0-9994432-0-0   (paperback)
ISBN 978-0-9994432-2-4   (ebook)

Contents

Introduction

The Foundation to Promote Personal Responsibility is a national, fiscally conservative, nonpartisan grassroots organization, whose objective is to support the return of our country's traditional values of self-reliance, self-determination, self-actualization, and social responsibility.

Our primary agenda is to put America onto a better fiscal path - - eliminate the curse of constant deficit spending and its potentially devastating effect on future generations (our children and grandkids). We have provided a link to the US debt clock, which shows that in October 2015, the amount of federal government debt per person (including minor children and retirees receiving Social Security) was in excess of $53,000 per citizen (and rising). The following link is to the live US debt clock, which show how much this amount has risen since October 2013.

http://www.usdebtclock.org/

We believe that it is immoral to push our country's current issues, problems and debt onto future generations. Our governmental units need to "live within their means", just the same as any business (large or small) or any individual, or any family. Our agenda is to promote polices that will enable the federal government to eliminate deficit spending and then begin to pay off the country's incurred indebtedness over a reasonable period of time. Our Foundation fully supports the work of The Campaign to Fix the Debt. We have included the following link to The Campaign's website. We encourage you to visit their website for additional information on the federal government's growing debt problem.

http://www.fixthedebt.org/

Our Foundation's overriding philosophy is anchored to the guiding principles outlined in the Declaration of Independence and the US Constitution. We have provided a link to the text of the Declaration of Independence. We encourage you to re-read the full text, to refresh your memory as to why this is as pertinent today, as it was in 1776. To paraphrase... The Declaration states that all people have certain unalienable rights, which include life, liberty and the pursuit of happiness. It also state that governments are instituted by its citizens and a government derives its power from the consent of the governed. However, when the government itself becomes destructive to these ends, it is the right (and responsibility) of the people to alter it, in order to maximize their personal safety and happiness.

https://www.varsitytutors.com/earlyamerica/declaration-independence

Our Editorial Board also subscribes to the wisdom put forth by a number of influential thought leaders, including those from the past, and in our Conversation Pieces, we will provide links to other works that will help our Foundation's membership appreciate how we can apply that wisdom in an addressing our country's issues.

Our Foundation's agenda also includes putting forth recommendations regarding government spending, tax reform, federal tax reduction, and term limits. We support evolutionary change. It took us a long time to get to the "current state", and it will take a period of time to move to a better "desired state".

Our Foundation's goals are to support the changes that maximize personal freedom and prosperity, balanced with each individual's Personal Responsibility to his-/herself and their family and fellow citizens.

Government / Politics

The foundation upon which the federal government is built is spelled out in the US Constitution. Our citizens' primary unalienable rights are specified in the first ten amendments to the Constitution, commonly referred to as The Bill of Rights. We have provided the links below.

https://www.varsitytutors.com/earlyamerica/freedom-documents/u-s-constitution/constitution-united-states

https://www.varsitytutors.com/earlyamerica/freedom-documents/bill-rights/bill-rights-text-version

The US Constitution, along with all of its amendments, represents the current "social contract" between our country's citizens and our federal government. Because our Foundation supports evolutionary change, we support working through the political process to change the things within this contract that need to be fixed.

Interestingly, our Editorial Board has found very few things within the current written contract that need to be fixed. However, we also find that our country is faced with urgent profound issues that the general public agrees need to get fixed.

So..... What prevents the country from being able to effectively move forward in solving these problems within the existing structure? Our Editorial Board believes that the current state of the "political process" is under significant distress (commonly referred to as "gridlock"), due to a number of issues that need to be addressed. We believe the political process can be improved by addressing the following topics:

- Term Limits

- The role(s) of the federal government and the level of federal spending

- Tax Reform (Tax Rationalization and Federal Tax Reduction)

By addressing these issues, we can move forward with solving the federal government's annual deficit, which is simply the difference between the federal government's spending (outflows) versus the federal government's revenues (inflows from taxes).

The "Conversation Pieces" that we have posted on our website have been written to put forth our Foundation's ideas (and to solicit additional ideas) regarding the best policies to be pursued, to move us toward a better "desired state". We fully expect that the political and policy recommendations supported by our Foundation will evolve over time based on our members' input, so we encourage your feedback and suggestions - - your personal participation in the conversation(s) and the Foundation's process.

The 20th Century has been characterized as being the "American Century". The United States has been one of the most prosperous (and yes, most powerful) nations in the world, and at the same time, our citizens have enjoyed the most personal freedoms anywhere in the world. This has been accomplished primarily because of the solid foundation(s) upon which our country was founded.

However, we have strayed away from a number of our core values, including replacing "Personal Responsibility" with "government programs". Our Editorial Board believes that we must make the necessary changes, so that we can return to those policies that enhance all citizens' prosperity, and maximize all citizens' personal freedoms.

We provided the following links to your US Senators and members of the House of Representatives.

https://www.senate.gov/general/contact_information/senators_cfm.cfm

https://www.house.gov/representatives/

Social Issues

Our Editorial Board recognizes the following fact - - America is continuing to become a more diverse country. This diversity includes not only ethnic diversity, but also cultural (i.e., "values") diversity. We applaud this diversity -

- we view this as a natural by-product of being one of the most prosperous countries in the world, with substantial (and unalienable) personal freedoms. People want to live here. However, this diversity also contributes to much of the "noise" within the public discourse, and it has a significant effect on the country's political process.

We also recognize that there are not any "absolutes" in regards to many of these social issues, and that in most cases, there is no single "absolutely right" or single "absolutely wrong" answer to the issue.

Our "Join the Conversation" page includes our Editorial Board's thoughts on a number of current social issues. Our Editorial Board's belief is that the conversation about most of these social issues can be conducted within the context of Personal Responsibility (and personal rights, choices and freedoms) versus a government program.

As we noted above, our Editorial Board does not feel that there are any major changes that need to be made to the social contract between our country's citizens and our federal government (the US Constitution) other than to impose fiscal restraints on the federal government, limit the power and jurisdiction of the federal government, and limit the terms of office for its officials and for members of Congress.

The members of our Editorial Board are strong supporters of the Bill of Rights –

- The First Amendment, which addresses religious freedoms, freedom of speech and the Press, and the Rights of the citizenry to assemble and petition the government to address any grievances

- The Second Amendment, which addresses the Right to bear arms

- The Fourth Amendment, which addresses the Rights of the citizenry to be secure against unreasonable searches and seizures

- And the Tenth Amendment, which specifies that powers not delegated to the federal government by the Constitution, are reserved to the states and (as applicable) to the people themselves.

In regards to the Tenth Amendment, you will note our Editorial Board has put forth a number of Conversation Pieces on what the scope of the federal government should be, and what should be moved to the states, or to local governmental units, or the private sector, or be addressed by Personal Responsibility (rather than another government program).

Our Editorial Board believes that our country is currently where we're at (at this point in time in our history) and we got here with the "best of intentions". Do we need to fix some things? Yes (this is what the political process is all about). Are there any "absolute right(s)" and "absolute wrong(s)"? No - But the country needs to make some tough decisions now (not later) in order to move towards a better "desired state". Do each of us have a Personal Responsibility to participate in the process? Our Editorial Board believes so. We encourage you to Join the Conversation.

Conversation Pieces

Why Mitt Romney's Comments about the 47% Were Not Correct

As you may recall, one of issues that arose during the 2012 presidential election was in regards to the following comments made by Mitt Romney at a fund raising event held in May of 2012 -

"There are 47% of the people who will vote for the president no matter what. All right, there are 47% who are with him, who are dependent upon government, who believe that they are victims, who believe the government has a responsibility to care for them, who believe that they are entitled to healthcare, to food, to housing, to you-name-it. That's an entitlement. The government should give it to them. And they will vote for this president no matter what. And I mean the president starts off with 48, 49...he starts off with a huge number. These are people who pay no income tax. Forty-seven percent of Americans pay no income tax. So our message of low taxes doesn't connect. So he'll be out there talking about tax cuts for the rich. ... My job is not to worry about those people. I'll never convince them they should take personal responsibility and care for their lives. What I have to do is convince the 5–10% in the center that are independents, that are thoughtful, that look at voting one way or the other depending upon in some cases emotion, whether they like the guy or not."

Keep in mind that Mr. Romney's comments were made at a political / fund raising event, where he was speaking "informally" (without a teleprompter) so there were a few incomplete (and somewhat incoherent) sentences, along with a number of comments that were not fully explained. The "political damage" that Mr. Romney inflicted upon himself was caused by his characterizing 47% of Americans as people who believe that they are victims and who believe the government has a responsibility to care for them, and that his "job" [as a presidential candidate? / as a future president?] was not to worry about those 47%.

Our Editorial Board feels that the percentage of Americans who feel that they are victims, and who feel that the federal government has a responsibility to care for them is a much smaller number, one that is not statistically relevant (probably less than 5 percent). We also believe that a substantial majority of people (probably over 80% of the people in both the Democratic and Republican parties) are concerned about the federal government's annual deficit, and the country's cumulative debt, and the breakdown of the country's political process in regards to the country's finances.

Mr. Romney's comments about entitlements were also wrong (and yet very correct). Under the Declaration of Independence, people have an unalienable right to life [along with liberty and the pursuit of happiness]. However, nowhere in our country's social contract (the US Constitution) does it state that the federal government has a responsibility to provide the essentials for everyday life – i.e., healthcare, food, housing, etc. The Constitution does state that We-the-People agree to "promote the general welfare" of the country's citizens, but nowhere does it state that the responsibility of the federal government is to provide the essentials for everyday life.

Our Editorial Board believes that there are a number of proper and essential roles for the government (which we discuss elsewhere on our website), however, most aspects of daily life should be handled personally. Our Foundation's primary goal is to promote Personal Responsibility. Another one of our Foundation's goals is to work towards shrinking the size of the federal government, and to help the government focus on its core responsibilities.

Tax Reform (Tax Rationalization and Federal Tax Reduction)
"The only things certain in life are death and taxes." – Benjamin Franklin

Keep in mind that Benjamin Franklin made this observation back in the 1700's (well before the federal government implemented the Federal Income Tax in 1913 via the 16th Amendment).

It is probably safe to say that no one "enjoys" paying taxes, especially when the daily press continues to report on various "inequities" and "special tax breaks" and how the federal government's tax system needs to be simplified and "reformed". However, before we can move forward with tax reform, we need to have a conceptual framework to address the various issues. Our Editorial Board uses the term "Tax Rationalization" as the main underpinning for this framework.

When you consider Federal Income taxes, Social Security and Medicare taxes, State Income Taxes, Federal and State estate taxes, Real Estate Taxes, Sales Tax on Purchases, etc. you begin to see that the conceptual framework needs to be fairly comprehensive. Having said that.... our Editorial Board believes that while our country's current framework for collecting tax dollars at the federal, state and local level can be (and should be) improved, it is generally OK. That's because, with each level of government that We-the-People have instituted, we create a governmental entity that needs its own "lifeblood" (ie, tax revenues) to fulfill the charter that we give to that institution to fulfill.

However, our Editorial Board also has specific thoughts and recommendations regarding the proper role(s) of government at the federal, state and local levels. So the first "tax rationalization" question becomes – Do we need a "government program" for a particular issue, or is this something that I (as an individual) should take Personal Responsibility to handle? Also - can the issue (service) be handled by a Not-for-Profit organization, instead of a government program?

When we do conclude that the issue is something that needs to be handled by a governmental entity (ie, fire protection, libraries, streets, national defense, etc) then we need to determine "by whom". Our belief is that issues are best handled locally, and then, if necessary, at the state level, and then (lastly) at the federal government level. In the conversation piece entitled *What the Government Should (and Should Not) Do* we talk about what we believe the proper (and very limited) role of the federal government should be.

The final piece of tax rationalization (once you have decided that an issue requires a federal government program) then becomes - what is the "best" (fairest) means of raising the necessary tax revenue. Unfortunately, this is a difficult part of the political process, because there will never be 100% agreement on the answer to the "fairness" question.

So let's step back, and first put forth some general points of agreement for any tax framework. The first basic principle is that everyone is a citizen and therefore everyone has a stake in (and an obligation to contribute towards) the government programs that We-the-People have voted to implement. The second basic principle is that we recognize each person's contribution should take into consideration their ability to pay. A key aspect of this principle is that those individuals in society who have benefited the most from our country's freedoms, economic system, and system of government, generally have an enhanced ability to pay, and therefore should pay a relatively higher portion of the taxes that are needed to fund the federal government programs that We-the-People have decided are necessary.

8

Let's pause here and set the remainder of the stage for the tax rationalization discussion. As we noted above, our Editorial Board has a very narrow definition of the proper role of the federal government. Accordingly (by definition) federal taxes will go down as programs and responsibilities are pushed down from the federal level, to the state level (if appropriate) or to the local level (if appropriate), or to the Personal Responsibility level.

Our Editorial Board also supports the concept of graduated income tax rates, whereby those citizens who have the most "*current year funds available*" (i.e, taxable income) contribute a relatively higher portion of the total tax revenues needed to operate the federal government. Our Foundation's primary focus is the federal government's Annual Deficit and Cumulative Debt, so the funding of state and local programs is somewhat beyond the scope of what our Editorial Board would like to address. However, we support the concepts of "fairness", along with an all- inclusive Personal Responsibility of each citizen to contribute towards their state and local government programs as well.

… which brings us back to one last key tax issue - the concept of Other People's Money (OPM). Let's first talk about Social Security and Medicare taxes. We have separate Conversation Pieces on the roles of these two federal government programs. In those Conversation Pieces, we discuss the fact that one of the end results of any government tax program is the redistribution of wealth. The primary end result of these two federal government programs is a transfer of wealth (which happens every year) between different generations of tax payers. However, in regards to the "tax rationalization" of Social Security and Medicare, we feel that this intergenerational transfer of wealth is generally accepted to be OK, as long as people are not misled to believe that Social Security is a pension plan, and Medicare is a health insurance policy. Instead, these programs merely represent an ongoing long term "social contract" between generations of citizens, and the associated wealth transfer is handled each year within the cash flows of the federal government.

However, one of the most significant problems that our Editorial Board has with our elected officials (at both the federal level and the state level) is that they have a tendency to extend this "intergenerational" concept to the remainder of all other federal and state government programs. Our Editorial Board feels that it is an immoral act of our elected officials to push the cost of today's programs onto future generations via the use of government debt. We-the-People need to re-engage in the political process, to ensure that our governmental units are "living within their means", in the same way that each of us attempts to take Personal Responsibility for our own personal lives and personal finances.

Government Spending – What the Federal Government Should (and Should Not) Do

We have a separate Conversation Piece that discusses the federal government's annual deficit, and in that Piece we provide a high level summary of the federal government's budgeted inflows (ie, tax revenues) and outflows (spending) for fiscal 2013. In that Conversation Piece we discuss specific categories of spending and the associated amounts. The purpose of this Conversation Piece is to discuss (at a conceptual level) the role(s) of government at the federal, state and local level.

As we have noted elsewhere, we believe that a governmental function is only appropriate in those situations where there is an issue that cannot be handled at the personal level, or by a nongovernmental (Not-for-Profit) organization. The federal government is not a nanny - people need to take Personal Responsibility for their own lives.

Further, we believe that the primary (and only) role of the federal government is to protect US citizens. Period. It is interesting to note that in Federalist Paper No. 30 – Concerning the General Power of Taxation, the first government function listed is support of the national forces (national defense) - - raising forces, building and equipping fleets, and all other expenses relating to military arrangements and operations.

Many people misinterpret the intent of one phrase in the opening sentence of the US Constitution, regarding what is meant by "promote the general Welfare" of its citizens. Accordingly, this misinterpretation has led some people to believe that dispensing welfare payments to individual citizens is one of the roles of the federal government. Our Editorial Board believes that the delivery of "social services" (welfare) to an individual is not a proper role of the government (federal or state), and cash welfare payments should not be provided by the US or state governments. The proper role of the federal government is to protect its citizens and promote the *general* good.

The best vehicle(s) for dispensing "social services" (welfare) to an individual (or a family who needs it) is a religious organization or a Not-for-Profit organization, which can specialize in providing a specific social service. The federal government can promote the general welfare of the people by supporting these religious and Not-for-Profit organizations, and that type of support can be provided via the country's tax policies (see *Tax Reform / Tax Simplification*).

10

It should be noted that "protection" does extend beyond purely military matters - - and in that regard, there is an appropriate role for the federal government in establishing and maintaining regulatory functions. Having said that, our Editorial Board believes that all federal regulatory activities should be analyzed, discussed / debated, and (if appropriate) approved, following a rigorous cost / benefit analysis. We recognize that in any analysis of costs versus benefits, there will inevitably be "soft dollar assumptions" on the perceived benefits to be derived from any regulatory activity. However, the cost of a regulatory activity can be specifically budgeted in a fairly straight forward manner. The proponents of any new regulatory initiative should be required to make their case (to convince the legislature) that the benefits of the regulation exceed the cost. In addition, the funding for any new proposed regulatory activity needs to be specifically identified in the legislation. If appropriate a new directed "user fee" should be part of the proposed legislation, so that the cost of the regulatory activity can be attached to the specific parties, rather than simply being covered by "general tax receipts" (that type of funding approach simply serves to avoid accountability).

We further recommend that the federal government's role is to write legislation on what the (minimum) federal regulations need to be. We further believe that there are (limited) instances where the actual regulatory activities will be performed by the federal government. However, for the majority of regulatory issues, the process of setting more stringent state regulations (beyond the federal minimums) and the actual execution of the regulatory function should be performed at the state level.

Federal Spending (in Billions)	Federal Budget	Mandatory	Discretionary	Alternative Budget	
Social Security	866	860	5	860	To diminish over time
Defense	627	9	618	627	OK / To be reviewed
Income Security	542	475	67	1	(to states and NFPOs)
Medicare	531	524	7	1	(to states and NFPOs)
Health	443	385	58	1	(to states and NFPOs)
Interest	223	223	0	223	
Veterans	148	86	62	148	Any reduction TBD
Education, training, Social Services	129	32	97	1	(to states and NFPOs)
Transportation	104	9	94	1	(to states and NFPOs)
Justice	59	16	43	59	Any reduction TBD
International Affairs	56	0	56	56	Any reduction TBD
Natural Resources / Environment	40	3	37	1	(to states and NFPOs)
Community & Regional Development	35	2	32	1	(to states and NFPOs)
Science, Space and Technology	30	0	30	1	(to states and NFPOs)
General Government	29	10	19	29	Any reduction TBD
Agriculture	23	17	7	1	(to states and NFPOs)
Energy	13	3	9	1	(to states and NFPOs)
Spending	3,898	2,654	1,241	2,012	
Revenues	3,030			3,012	**
Annual (Deficit)/Surplus	(868)	-29%	*	1,000	***

* We have a fundamental question -
What kind of business (or individual or family) can
successfully stay afloat under a recurring annual 29% deficit?

** A slight reduction in total tax receipts

*** Goal: A $1 trillion surplus, to begin paying
down the Cumulative Debt over the
next 17 years or so

TBD - To Be Determined

NFPOs – Not-for-Profit Organizations

October 2013

Tax Reform / Tax Simplification

Tithing is an Old Testament concept. The tithe was a requirement of the law in which all Israelites were to give 10 percent of everything they earned and grew to the Temple. The New Testament does not designate a percentage of income that a person should set aside, but only says that the amount contributed should be "in keeping with income" – – we should give as we are able.

Our Editorial Board agrees with the tithing concepts noted above, and we feel that these concepts should also apply in regards to our country's federal income tax policies for personal income tax returns. Each citizen, as a member of society, has an obligation to financially support the operations of the various federal governmental units that the citizenry has agreed to establish and maintain. We also agree that tax policies should take into consideration each person's ability to pay, and we feel that it is appropriate that the lowest tax bracket currently in effect for federal income tax purposes for the initial tranche of taxable income is the 10% tax bracket.

However, in moving towards a more simplified system of taxation, one of the first questions that needs to be addressed is the 6.2% Social Security tax and 1.45% Medicare tax that is withheld from wages. We have a separate Conversation Piece on both Social Security and Medicare. As we note in those pieces, the tax withholdings and benefit payments that are made under these two programs are simply an annual transfer of wealth from one group of citizens to another. Accordingly, we feel that people should get credit for these tax withholdings in calculating their federal income tax obligation.

Our Conversation Piece on Medicare also provides additional details on how "universal healthcare" (which is a laudable goal) should be accomplished (managed) and paid for in the future.

The goal of "tax simplification" has been debated for years. However, the only thing that seems to happen each year is that new tax code sections are written and added to the federal tax code, to make the tax system even more complex. Don't get us wrong – many of the tax code changes that have been passed each year were put forward with the best of intentions, to address and "solve" some particular issue.

However, our Editorial Board feels that this "tampering of the marketplace" is not healthy for the economy – – each of these tax preferences serves to distort the marketplace. For example, let's discuss one of the oldest "sacred cows" –

the tax deduction for mortgage interest. As you may recall, many years ago, people could take an itemized deduction for any type of interest expense (ie, car loans, credit cards, etc). Then changes to the tax code were implemented whereby the interest expense deduction was limited to only mortgage interest and home equity line of credit interest. So, what did people do? If they needed to borrow money for a car, and they had built up equity in their home, they took out a home equity loan to finance their car, so they accomplished the same end result that the legislature was trying to eliminate. But the real question was - why were those people given an advantage in comparison to some young college kid, who also needed a car, but was renting an apartment? While the dream of home ownership continues to be a laudable goal, should the federal government "subsidize" homeowners, at the expense of those people who rent?

Similarly, is there any reason why income from investments (ie, "capital gains") be taxed differently than income from wages? Income is income. One of the major downsides of the current "tax preference" for capital gains (or any similar "tax preference" item) is that this "tax break" contributes towards the level of resentment between the "have nots" and the "haves".

Having said all that.... Our Editorial Board believes that it is "probably" OK for the federal government to propose and implement a limited number of tax incentives for business income tax purposes. Accordingly, at this point in time, we are not going to put forth any recommendations to simplify the tax code as it relates to the taxation of business enterprises. Our Foundations focus in on promoting Personal Responsibility, and we want to focus on Personal Responsibility versus relying on a government program.

We believe that the country can vastly simplify the tax system for personal income tax returns. The attached "illustrative examples" show our recommendations for The New 1040 Form.

Our Editorial Board agrees with the position taken by the Campaign to Fix the Debt - - until the federal government can restructure its operations (both spending and tax revenues) to eliminate deficit spending and begin repaying the cumulative US debt, we need to support both spending reductions and (at least during the near term) increases in tax collections. We feel that the tax simplification changes illustrated on the accompanying New 1040 Form represent the most simple and most "fair" proposal that we can recommend.

Please note the following key concepts, along with their rationale –

14

We do not see a need to change the definition of gross income to be included on a taxpayer's federal income tax return. Income is income, and all gross income should continue to be reported on a taxpayer's federal tax return.

For personal tax returns, all "tax breaks" (tax preference items) should be eliminated. We recommend that only three deductions be allowed to arrive at income that is subject to income tax.

We believe that it is the Personal Responsibility of each individual to set aside their own funds for their retirement years. See our Conversation Piece on Social Security. As we all know, it was never intended that a person's social security benefits would be the sole source of their retirement income. Accordingly, we support the continuation of the existing rules, whereby a certain portion of current year income can be set aside in an IRA or 401K plan and excluded from the taxpayer's current year taxable income.

The federal government should also not tax income that is needed for basic sustenance. We may need to re-visit how the federal government calculates the "federal poverty guideline" amounts, but this portion of a taxpayer's income should be excluded from taxable income.

With the recent passage of legislation to implement universal healthcare coverage, the cost of healthcare should also be excluded from taxable income. Whether this amount is shown separately, or if this amount gets incorporated into the Federal Poverty Guideline amount, we can decide that issue later. But the deduction should be the minimum "federal standard" (bronze level) amount. If someone wants to acquire a more comprehensive (and more expensive) healthcare policy, incurring that additional cost would be their own personal decision, but the incremental cost would not be a deductible cost. You will also note that if a taxpayer does not acquire a healthcare policy, the Supreme Court has ruled that this cost has now become a federally sanctioned tax, and therefore, this amount will be paid to the IRS by the taxpayer when they file their federal income tax return.

The next section of the attached schedule is a conceptual illustration of possible progressive tax brackets. Further analysis needs to be done by the government to determine if the resulting tax revenues will be adequate to cover the current cost of running the government, and also supply a surplus that can be used to begin paying down the cumulative US debt. Obviously, the tax rates and income ranges cannot be set in advance, until federal government spending has been re-structured and spending reductions have been put into place. Our recommendation to the federal government is - - DO THE MATH - - structure the federal government's costs and revenues, so that the federal government starts living within its means, and so that We-the-People can begin to pay down the federal government's cumulative debt.

Lastly, you will note that the 6.2% social security tax and the 1.45% Medicare tax will be used to satisfy a portion of the taxpayer's annual tithing requirement. Also, as you will note in the Conversation Piece on *Medicare and Universal Health Care Coverage*, the amounts collected by the federal government for Medicare taxes would be repaid directly back to the applicable state from where the tax was withheld. It will be the responsibility of the state(s) (via the state's health insurance exchange and Medicare receipts) to provide healthcare coverage to their state's citizens.

As we have noted elsewhere, over the past several years, the federal government has built up a substantial cumulative debt amount that needs to be repaid. For the next several years, tax revenues will need to increase in the short term, until this cumulative debt amount has been repaid. Accordingly, you will note that our recommendation is to implement a 40% tax bracket and a 49% tax bracket. Our Editorial Board supports the concept of progressive tax rates, even though these rates are higher than what we would generally support, if we were not faced with the cumulative US debt.

As we noted above, citizens should "give" based upon their ability to do so. Also, the government should not tax income that is needed for daily living expenses. However, once a person's income rises above that minimal level, those individuals and families who have reaped the benefits of living in a country that has been structured to maximize personal freedoms and wealth accumulation are in the best position to support the operations of their country.

It should be noted that in the past (during times of significant "collective stress") the top marginal tax rate has been significantly higher than what we are recommending on the attached schedule. During World War I, the top marginal tax rate was 77%. This rate gradually decreased, but in 1939 during the Great Depression, the top marginal tax rate was once again increased to 75%. The maximum rate occurred during World War II when the top marginal tax rate in 1944 and 1945 was 94%. As recently as the years 1981 through 1986 the top tax rate was 50%. The reason we are recommending the implementation of a top marginal tax rate of 49% is symbolic - - we feel that if a person gets to keep 51% of what they earn, then they are still working for themselves, rather than working for the federal government.

So, what is the trade-off for people who are faced with these higher tax rates? We are recommending that taxpayers get a tax credit for their contributions to

federal, state and local charities. As we have noted elsewhere, our Editorial
Board does not believe that governmental units should provide cash welfare
payments to individuals. At the same time, there is always going to be a need
for society to help those who are in need – and that is a role that religious
organizations and Not-for-Profit organizations are in the best position to
fulfill. To support these organizations, people who would otherwise be
making a large tax payment to the federal government will have the option to
direct some of their tax payment to the charity(s) of their choice. This is a
change from current tax policy, where contributions to charities are an
itemized deduction that reduces taxable income. Under current tax policies,
the "tax benefit" of a charitable contribution for a person in the top tax bracket
is 39.6% of the amount contributed. We are recommending a 50% tax credit
for contributions to state and local charities, religious organizations, etc, and a
100% tax credit for federally designated charities. Examples of federally
designated charities could be the American Red Cross, Habitat for Humanity,
a federal food bank, etc.

Our Foundation's goal / intention is that once the federal government has re-
structured its spending, and once We-the-People have repaid our cumulative
US debt obligations, the top tax bracket would begin to be reduced below 49%
(perhaps to a level no more than a top tax bracket of 30%).

The New 1040	Single person	Family of four	Family of four	Family of four	
Four Illustrative Examples					
Wages	30,000	65,000	200,000	1,000,000	
Interest and dividends	100	200	200	10,000	
Pensions and Social Security	0	0	0	0	
Investment gains/losses	0	500	1,000	45,000	
Business Income (K-1s etc)	0	0	0	250,000	
Total Gross Income	30,100	65,700	201,200	1,305,000	(No change from current 1040)
Deductions -					
401Ks / IRAs	2,000	4,000	4,000	4,000	(Meeting personal responsibility / No change from current 1040)
Federal Poverty Guideline Amount	11,490	23,550	23,550	23,550	(Meeting personal responsibility)
Std Federal Health Insurance Amount *	4,000	9,000	9,000	9,000	(Meeting personal responsibility)
Total Deductions	17,490	36,550	36,550	36,550	
Taxable Income	**12,610**	**29,150**	**164,650**	**1,268,450**	
Federal Income Tax -					
10% Tax Bracket	1,261	2,500	2,500	2,500	First $25,000
20% Tax Bracket	0	830	15,000	15,000	$25,000 to $100,000
30% Tax Bracket	0	0	19,395	45,000	$100,000 to $250,000
40% Tax Bracket	0	0	0	300,000	$250,000 to $1,000,000
49% Tax Bracket	0	0	0	131,541	Over $1,000,000
Total Tax	1,261	3,330	36,895	494,041	
Blended Effective Tax Rate -					
On Gross Income	4%	5%	18%	38%	
On Taxable Income	10%	11%	22%	39%	
Settlement Thereof -					
6.2% Social Security withheld	1,860	4,030	12,400	62,000	
1.45% Medicare withheld	435	943	2,900	14,500	
Tax (refund from) / payment to IRS	(1,034)	(1,643)	(905)	395,041	
100% Tax Credit for Contributions to Federally designated Charities	0 **	0 **	15,000	15,000	Say $15,000
50% Tax Credit for Contributions to State and Local Charities	0 **	0 **	7,500	7,500	Say $15,000
	1,261	3,330	36,895	494,041	
			905 **		
			37,800		

* The insurance premium amounts shown are illustrative only - these premium amounts will be provided by the government once the health insurance exchanges have been established, and these "bronze level" premiums have been established.

   If "proof of purchase" is not provided, this amount would be paid to the IRS on the tax return, in keeping with the Supreme Court ruling that the purchase of healthcare is a federally mandated tax

** Charitable contributions would need to be a non-refundable tax credit. There will also need to be a limit (to be determined) on the maximum percentage of an individual's/ family's tax obligation that could be offset by charitable contributions.

Social Security - - A Ponzi Scheme (?)

A Ponzi scheme is an illegal financial scheme (i.e., a scam) named after Charles Ponzi, who pleaded guilty on November 1, 1920 of bilking millions of dollars from his investors for his own personal financial gain. In this type of scheme, proceeds from a second group of "investors" are used to pay the promised benefits to the initial group of investors (along with a certain portion of the proceeds being skimmed off and paid to the perpetrator of the scam), and then proceeds from the third group of investors are used to pay the second group, and so on, until the scam eventually collapses in on itself. These scams happen periodically, and one of the most recent examples of a Ponzi scheme is the scam that was run by Bernie Madoff (for his own personal gain) in the years up through 2008.

OK – Social Security is not a Ponzi scheme - - it is not being run by an individual for their own personal gain, and it's not illegal. Actually, it is a federally sanctioned program that was enacted into law in 1935.

So, is Social Security a 401K plan? Sort of, but not really. It's true that wages are being withheld from your pay check, and you don't see that portion of your wages in your take home net pay. However, you don't have a specific account at the Social Security Administration, where your actual Social Security withholdings are being deposited, invested and tracked, so that they can be repaid to you specifically, dollar for dollar, plus the related investment earnings once you retire. It is true that you do have an account with the Social Security Administration, but when you start receiving benefits, those benefits are not directly tied to the specific amounts that you paid in - - the total benefit amount that you ultimately receive may be less, or it may be more than what you paid in.

Because of the way benefits are paid to recipients, Social Security is more like a defined benefit pension plan. However, the key difference between Social Security and a corporate-sponsored pension plan is that corporations are required to actuarially determine the value of those future benefits that have been promised, and are required to set aside the proper amount of funds into a separate legal entity, and those specific funds are then used only to pay those defined benefits. The requirement to fund those future obligations each year, and to segregate those specific assets, is the key difference between a corporate pension plan and Social Security.

It is true that there are actuarial valuations performed each year to determine the present value of what the federal government has promised to pay in the future, along with a determination of the amount that has not yet been funded into the Social Security system. This debt obligation amount as of the country's September 30, 2012 fiscal yearend has been estimated to be an additional debt of $11.3 trillion, which is separate from (and in addition to) the explicit debt amount that is shown on the balance sheet of the federal government. This $11.3 trillion "off balance sheet" debt is the amount pertaining to the Social Security program only. If you were to go ahead and record a similar debt obligation for the actuarially determined obligation of future Medicare benefits, the amount for Medicare is even worse – an additional debt amount of $37.2 trillion for Medicare. Please see our separate Conversation Piece entitled *Medicare and Universal Health Coverage* for additional thoughts and recommendations in regards to healthcare costs.

So…. What exactly is Social Security, if it's not a Ponzi scheme or a legitimate pension plan? Our Editorial Board's characterization of Social Security is that it is simply a "social contract" that is facilitated by and administered by the federal government between generations of citizens. Social Security is not a funded retirement plan with separately segregated, invested assets that are the source of the funds to pay the promised benefits. Instead, Social Security merely represents a government-run program that facilitates an annual transfer of wealth from one generation of citizens to another group of citizens - - and that's OK, as long as people understand the true nature of this social contract, and they do not look at Social Security as being a pension plan. Accordingly, because the obligations / future benefits have not yet been funded, this is the reason for the concern about whether the country will be able to continue to pay the promised benefits in the future.

Because the country's annual Social Security benefit payments are being funded out of current year tax revenues, we believe that the withholding of Social Security taxes from current wages should be counted towards satisfying a taxpayer's obligation for federal income taxes. Please refer to our Conversation Piece entitled *Tax Reform / Tax Simplification* for further details.

Medicare and Universal Health Care Coverage

Hoo, boy… So, where do we begin? Maybe the best thing to do is first talk about the concept of insurance. As we get into the topic of Medicare and the Affordable Care Act (ACA) it might be best if we first talk about the conceptual nature of insurance and the similarities between health insurance and auto insurance. So, what is insurance, and why do you need it? First of all, you only need insurance when you need it. Otherwise, it's just a cash outflow. This is true for any kind of insurance, including auto insurance, homeowner's insurance, and health insurance. Over the years, there have been a number of drivers out there who have faithfully paid their auto insurance premiums every year of their driving lives, and never had a need to file a claim (or receive insurance proceeds from another driver who was at fault). For these drivers, auto insurance was simply just another cost of driving, similar to the cost of gas, tires and oil. But the state in which you live won't let you drive (legally) unless you've paid your auto insurance cost. So here is the true nature of auto insurance – you send some money (an insurance "tax") to an entity (an insurance company) - the insurance company can then use that money to make a payment to another counterparty (for example, another insured motorist) who might otherwise have been financially wiped out if they also didn't have auto insurance coverage.

Another general insurance issue (and marketplace concept) is that there are different levels of costs for different levels of coverage. That is what the insurance market place is all about. That is what choice is all about. (We'll come back to this later).

Contrary to popular belief (ie, that universal healthcare coverage is an "entitlement") once the ACA was passed by Congress and then signed into law by President Obama on March 23, 2010, the true nature of universal healthcare coverage became clear – health insurance is now a mandated "tax" (like auto insurance). With the Supreme Court's landmark decision regarding the "individual mandate" provision of the ACA, every citizen must now obtain healthcare coverage, or they have to pay a tax/penalty to the IRS if they don't otherwise make arrangements to be covered under an employer's healthcare plan or obtain coverage through their state's health insurance exchange.

Prior to the passage of the ACA and the Supreme Court ruling, obtaining health coverage had been optional. To some degree, it still is. Under federal law, if you are a young healthy 20-something-year old who just moved out of your parents' home, and you want to roll the dice that you won't get sick, you are not required to buy health insurance. However (starting in 2014) you will need to include some amount on your federal income tax return to pay for your lack of health insurance coverage.

Having said all that…. It is the belief of our Editorial Board that universal healthcare coverage is a laudable goal. There is some merit to the following statement, which was distributed by the Treasury Department - *The individual mandate guarantees personal responsibility. Without it, there's nothing to prevent people from only buying health insurance when they need it – which is similar to allowing people to buy homeowners insurance when their house is on fire.*

Prior to the passage of the ACA, it was reported that 49.9 million citizens (over 16% of the population) were not covered by health insurance during 2010, either due to a conscious decision to not acquire coverage, or due to an individual's lack of available funds to acquire affordable coverage. In some ways, it was a national embarrassment that a certain portion of the population who could afford coverage, decided to avoid Personal Responsibility, and instead intended to rely upon a government program (or the benevolence of their extended family or fellow citizens) to help them out in the event that they encountered a serious medical issue.

Our Editorial Board believes that the procurement of healthcare coverage is an act of Personal Responsibility (for yourself and to your family). We also understand the similarities with the government's requirement that you acquire auto insurance, which is needed because you are insuring against a risk that in the event of an accident, you could be affecting someone else's life and future financial situation. Conversely, home owners insurance is not mandated, because the government allows you to roll the dice in regards to the risk of fire, etc. (that is unless you are required to have homeowners insurance because you still have a mortgage loan against your home, in which case, you are really covering your lender's risk).

The connections that we are making in regards to health insurance is that nearly everyone (including the uninsured) could get their immediate trauma medical needs administered to them "free of charge" in the local Emergency Room at the local hospital. However, if that were to be the primary delivery mechanism for healthcare services in the country, the rest of the population would still end up paying for the cost of that care through higher insurance premiums.

Having said all of that.... Our Editorial Board is appalled that this complex social (and Personal Responsibility) issue is now formally under the management of the federal government. (Cue up the "Highway to Hell" soundtrack).

In June 2012 the White House issued a press release after the Supreme Court ruled that health insurance is a "tax". There are three statements in the press release that we take exception to –

The Affordable Care Act includes numerous provisions to keep healthcare costs low. Someone in the administration needs to define "low". Due to the definitional nature of insurance (along with other taxes and other wealth transfer schemes) someone's "low" ends up being someone else's "high". The only way to decrease the overall aggregate level of cost for the country's annual healthcare bill lies within the medical community itself and in the free market. (We are not going to go into a discussion about ambulance chasers, medical litigation, the medical profession's excessive testing just to cover themselves against potential litigation, etc. and the resulting effects on healthcare costs).

Over 86 million Americans have gained from coverage of preventive care free of charge, like mammograms for women and wellness visits for seniors. There is no such thing as a free lunch (or free coverage) - - someone (else) is paying for these preventive care services. It's true that these particular 86 million people received these services free of charge, but other people have borne the cost. This is just another form of taxes / wealth transfer.

Millions of Americans will soon be eligible for tax credits to ensure that their health insurance is affordable. We are opposed to any expansion of the list of "tax preference items" that distort the marketplace. Instead, we are putting forth a number of recommendations (see below) on how healthcare should be handled for federal income tax purposes, which do not distort the marketplace or expand the list of government "entitlements".

Our Editorial Board does agree with the following statements in the press release –
....families will get the security they deserve and (ACA) protects every American from the worst insurance company abuses. As we have noted elsewhere on our website, the appropriate regulation of the capitalistic marketplace is an appropriate role for the federal government.

States can also implement their own brand of reform through Innovation..... If States can come up with even better ways of covering people at the same quality and low cost, this law allows them to do so. We are relieved to hear that much of the restructuring of the country's healthcare system is going to be handled at the state level, rather than the federal level. Our hope is that once a particular state (and the health insurance companies operating within that state) have figured out the best way to handle this federal mandate, those "best practices" ideas can be shared with other states, so that the benefits of the capitalistic system (ie, products and services at the lowest prices available) can spread from one insurance company to another, and from one state to another.

In regards to Medicare..... Similar to Social Security, this federal program is simply a program to help facilitate the transfer of wealth from one generation (of currently working employees) to another (previous) generation. And that's OK - as long as people understand that this is simply the existing "social contract" between generations, and We-the-People are not misled into thinking that Medicare is a health insurance program. The simple reason Medicare is not a health insurance policy is that insurance companies insure risks, and they set premiums accordingly. Therefore, the annual health insurance premium for a 20-something person would be, say, $1,000 per year, and an annual health insurance premium for an 80-year old would be, say, $25,000 per year.

So.... How should this vast pool of healthcare money be handled? First, the federal government should not administer or pay for healthcare. The federal government has done its job - it needs to continue to set appropriate federal regulations for healthcare, but healthcare needs to be administered at the state level. Accordingly, all Medicare payroll tax withholdings (ie, Medicare tax receipts) should continue to come into the federal government, and then be immediately repaid directly to the state where those withholdings have come from, so that the states have their funds to administer Medicare, Medicaid and healthcare costs. Similarly, all federal income tax receipts that come in on federal income tax returns for the tax/penalty from those people who have elected to not obtain health insurance should be immediately repaid directly to the state where those tax proceeds originated.

Now the hard part – - we need someone to do the math, and set the "federal standard cost" for healthcare for individuals and families. Please refer to the Conversation Piece entitled *Tax Reform / Tax Simplification*. In that piece we recommend that taxable income should be calculated after deducting "the cost of daily living expenses" which includes the cost of assuming Personal Responsibility for obtaining health insurance. Once these "federal standard cost" amounts have been established, it should be fairly simple to complete an income tax return. It should also be somewhat easy to determine whether someone has maintained coverage or not, and if not, pay the health insurance amount to the federal government, so that this "mandated tax" can be forwarded back to their home state.

One last thought on insurance premiums. There has been a lot of discussion about the state healthcare insurance exchanges, along with their insurance offerings and the associated costs. We recommend that the "federal standard cost" amounts be based on the cost of the "bronze level" of coverage. We feel that all citizens should have a minimum level of coverage to handle catastrophic losses. Beyond that level, it would be the Personal Responsibility of the individual to determine the cost versus benefit of signing up for a more comprehensive (and more costly) health insurance policy. That is what choice and Personal Responsibility is all about....

24
"Entitlements"

Life, Liberty and The Pursuit of Happiness - - That's it – the sum total of what is spelled out in the Declaration of Independence.

Of course, there are also the first ten amendments to the US Constitution (the Bill of Rights) - - These basic fundamental rights can also be considered to be entitlements.

One more…. We-the-People are also entitled to equal opportunities, and there is an appropriate role for the federal and the state governments to ensure equality of opportunities. Because our country is the "land of opportunity", equal opportunity is the default presumption. If an individual feels that equal opportunity is being denied, then they have the opportunity to pursue the matter with the assistance of the American Civil Liberties Union.

Our Editorial Board believes that these entitlements and basic rights are all that the federal government (or any governmental unit) is obligated to provide to its citizens – no less, and no more. We believe that anything beyond these entitlements and basic rights are a Personal Responsibility, and are something that a person needs to acquire for themselves.

But what about the necessities of daily life - - food, water, shelter, etc? Shouldn't the federal government provide these basic needs to its citizens? If so, the question becomes - what is the list of those items, and what price is the price? (See our Conversation Piece on *Capitalism, Communism and Socialism*). Also, doesn't a person's "needs" include a basic education? And what about healthcare?

Our Editorial Board believes that there are appropriate limitations in regards to what the federal government (or any other governmental unit) should provide to its citizens. Although this may sound harsh, the government is not (and should not be) a nanny, a fairy godmother, or a sugar daddy. Providing for the necessities of daily life is a Personal Responsibility.

Having said that…. We are also cognizant of the fact that for some citizens, acquiring the necessities of daily life can become a daily struggle. As we mention in the Conversation Piece on *Tax Reform / Tax Simplification*, we believe that religious organizations and Not-for-Profit organizations are the proper vehicles for addressing these citizens' needs, rather than a government program. Our Editorial Board believes that the country's citizens continue to be a very generous, civic-minded, and compassionate community, and in that Conversation Piece, we illustrate how the federal government and the country's taxpayers can support these religious and Not-for-Profit organizations via the country's federal income tax policies.

Who is Working for Who?

As you read through the Federalist Papers and the US Constitution, you get the clear impression that the original intent of the Founders was to establish a government that would be working *to form a more perfect union*, to carry out the will of its citizens.

So…. Why is the current approval rating for Congress so low? And because of the cumulative debt amount that the federal government has managed to run up, and the significant tax burdens that the government has put upon both the current and future generations, is it unreasonable that so many citizens now feel that they are working for the government, rather than the way it was originally intended?

Our Editorial Board believes that we are seeing the result of something that the Founders were concerned about from the very beginning. In Federalist Paper # 47 one of the important questions was whether any powers transferred to the federal government would be unnecessary or improper, and whether there might be a situation where that power would be perverted to the detriment of the public. Also, the title of Federalist Paper # 57 is *The Alleged Tendency of the New Plan to Elevate the Few at the Expense of the Many Considered in Connection with Representation,* and in that essay there was a warning about the potential for the sacrifices of the many (the public) being used for the *"aggrandizement"* of the few (ie, our elected representatives).

Let's pause, and make it clear that we totally support and applaud the concept of Public Service. We recognize that elected officials are putting themselves out there, suspending their private lives while campaigning for, and serving in public office, so that they can serve the public good. That was the original intent. However, this fear has always been there from the very beginning, that the "public good" can easily be supplanted with the "personal good" or self-aggrandizement of the elected official - whether it be for personal financial gain or simply for the intangible value of "power".

As we have noted elsewhere on our website, the primary recommendation that we are putting forth to counter the potential self-aggrandizement of the individual elected official (at the expense of the general public) is to implement term limits for all elected "executive" and "legislative" positions. We feel that there is a lot of wisdom in the 22nd Amendment - - We-the-People finally got smart, and amended the US Constitution, to implement term limits for the US President. We feel that this same type of wisdom should now also be applied to all elected "executive" and "legislative" positions at both the federal and state levels of government. Our Editorial Board also supports the concept put forth in the 22nd Amendment regarding one re-election possibility. This is the means by which We-the-People can provide our feedback to that individual on whether they have been effective in fulfilling their obligations and responsibilities to the citizens, and if appropriate, the citizens can choose to re-elect that individual. However, at the end of the second term of public service, we will say "thank you" to that individual, and ask them to go back to their personal life (which could include trying to get elected to a different federal or state government position). We no longer want to have an entrenched "entitled" government bureaucracy permanently holding on to elected positions. These executive and legislative positions are not "owned" by that individual, they are available to be "rented" to our elected officials for a maximum of two terms. We simply can't afford the status quo any longer.

Although our Editorial Board shares the concern expressed by the country's Founders regarding the possible self-aggrandizement of our elected officials, we are just as concerned about the aggrandizement of the bureaucracies that have been put into place to support our elected officials. We have this concern because we can clearly see the connections between the two. The "bureaucracies" are many - - the various federal and state agencies and "service departments", the public sector unions, and the various lobbyist organizations that seek to influence the policies of the federal and state governments.

Back in the days when many of our Editorial Board members were getting ready to graduate (whether from high school or from college) we were faced with some very fundamental personal decisions about what to do with our lives. Many years ago, part of those personal decisions included assessing whether we should enter the "private sector" or the "public sector". A key decision point has been, and always will be, financial. "Back then" the tradeoff was to enter the private sector and compete for the potentially higher (potentially unlimited) financial rewards of joining the capitalistic economic system, or to settle for a comparable (but lower paying position) in the public sector. Unfortunately, what has transpired over the past several years is that the "benefits" of public sector life have risen to the point where the private sector now feels like it is working for the public sector.

How did this happen? Well, first of all, it is very easy for our elected officials to support their bureaucracy(s) that put them into their (permanent) elected office to begin with. Second, it's very easy for our elected officials to spend

OPM (Other People's Money) rather than having to make the difficult financial decisions that people in the private sector need to deal with every day. And it is even easier for our elected officials to promise future guarantees to their bureaucracy(s) regarding future pension benefits that they don't even need to fund currently, as they can easily push these costs on to future generations.

Our Editorial Board has four recommendations. As mentioned above, our first recommendation is to institute Term Limits, so that We-the-People (not the bureaucracies) can elect people into executive and legislative positions, who are motivated to serve the Public Good, rather than the Personal Good.

The second recommendation is that our elected officials re-establish the differential between private sector pay and public service pay. When you consider the level of unemployment in the country (some of which can be attributed to the government's policies) it should not be a problem to continue to be able to find qualified people for governmental "service department" positions.

Our third recommendation is that elected "executive" officials manage their responsibilities like an executive in the private sector. Accordingly, they should come in to office with two objectives – to evaluate the processes and efficiencies of the service departments that will become their responsibility, and to evaluate the competency and effectiveness of the public sector employees in those departments. Candidates who are running for executive positions need to campaign on these two issues. They need to know what they're running for and they should also possess a knowledge of the governmental employees who will be working for them. If that candidate has a better idea on how to execute the responsibility of their office, that is the candidate the people should elect. Similarly, candidates running for legislative positions should campaign by stating what legislation they intend to pursue, to make the country (or their state) better. However, please see our conversation piece entitled *There ought to be a law (or not)*.

Our final recommendation is in regards to fixing the problems (and the "upside down" position) that we have managed to get ourselves into regarding the compensation and pension benefits of people employed in the public sector versus the private sector. Please see our Conversation Piece on *Governmental (Public) Pension Obligations*.

28
The Federal Government's Assets and Debts

Our Editorial Board has spent a substantial amount of time reviewing the federal government's annual "budget" (ie, the "annual deficit") along with the related Financial Statements of the federal government that are published by the US Department of the Treasury in cooperation with the Office of Management and Budget (OMB). The most current Financial Report of the federal government for the fiscal year ending on September 30, 2012, is available on the internet.

The purpose of this conversation piece is to provide our thoughts and observations on the federal government's Financial Statements. We have approached this exercise as business people who understand the nature of business, and the nature of the assets owned by an enterprise, along with that enterprise's obligations.

First - The "bad news" - - The assets owned by the federal government (as defined) total $2.7 trillion, and the liabilities owed by the federal government (as defined) total $18.8 trillion – therefore We-the-People are $16.1 trillion in the hole. Also, We-the-People need to keep in mind that foreign governments hold more than $4.5 trillion of this debt, and the largest foreign holder of US debt is China, which owns more than $1.2 trillion. (However, it can be argued – and it has been argued - both positively and negatively - that China's holding of US debt is a good thing.... or a bad thing). Having said that..... It doesn't matter who holds our debt paper - we believe that any federal government debt owed to anyone is a bad thing, because it means that the federal government is not living within its means.

Second – The "worse news" - - If you were to include "on book" the present value of unfunded intergenerational social obligations for Social Security and Medicare, the amount of the federal government's liabilities would increase by another $48.5 trillion, over and above the amount published in its annual report. (However, see our separate Conversation Pieces on Social Security and Medicare).

Third – The "worst news" - - We continue to head in the wrong direction at an accelerating pace. The budgeted deficit for 2013 (additional borrowing / debt) was another $868 billion. The table below tracks the cumulative government debt over the past 10 years (it is not going down) –

2003 - $6.8 trillion, 2004 - $7.4 trillion, 2005 - $7.9 trillion, 2006 - $8.5 trillion, 2007 - $9.0 trillion, 2008 - $10.0 trillion, 2009 - $11.9 trillion, 2010 - $13.5 trillion, 2011 - $14.8 trillion, 2012 - $16.1 trillion

Now, some good news - - The federal government's financial statements do not include all of the assets owned by the federal government. The value(s) of the following assets are nowhere to be found in the federal government's financial statements – the interstate highway system, national parks, other land owned by the federal government, etc. There is a footnote within the financial statements that indicates the "remaining depreciable net value" of certain military property, plant and equipment is included in the country's total assets, but a separate specific value for those military assets is not disclosed (appropriately), nor is there any way to determine what the "intrinsic useful value" of those type of assets might be. (Who can put a dollar figure on the true value of the country's nuclear deterrent?)

One last issue.... There is a generally accepted accounting concept regarding "intangible" assets (which include "goodwill"). You can look at goodwill as being the excess of favors bestowed versus favors received. Our Editorial Board believes that the country still maintains a little bit of positive goodwill that was banked with the French for D-Day (but you can never tell with the French). It is generally understood that the value of the country's goodwill goes up and down every day, depending on whether we're doing something good somewhere in the world, or if we're spying on our allies.

The bottom line is that the United States of America is far from being bankrupt - - we are certain that the value of what we have going for us exceeds our obligations. However, having said that.... The cumulative US debt is real and it must be addressed, which means that we need to re-structure the operations of the federal government, so that it not only lives within its means, but for a period of time over the next several years, the tax revenues of the federal government will need to exceed its spending, so that the current generation of responsible citizens can begin to pay down the existing US debt. This task must be undertaken by our generation – **not** our children's generation, and **not** our grandchildren's generation.

The Deficit and Current Cumulative Debt – The Timetable for the "Work-out"

We have prepared a separate Conversation Piece that discusses the federal government's spending, and in that piece we provide a summary of the budgeted deficit for 2013. We are certain that the country's founders would never have envisioned the day that the federal government would become the nation's largest creditor, debtor, lender, employer, consumer, contractor, grantor, property owner, tenant insurer, health-care provider and pension guarantor.

Here are some statistics regarding the trajectory of the growth in the scope of the federal government's spending, expressed as a percentage of the country's GDP (Gross Domestic Product) –

1887 – 2.4%, 1938 – 7.9%, 1983 – 22.9%, 2012 – 25.2%.

Not only is the magnitude of the federal government's spending on the wrong trajectory, our politicians (in both the executive and legislative branches of government) are failing the country's citizens by pushing the obligations for this spending on to future generations.

The amounts below show the growth in the country's cumulative "on book" debt over the past 10 years –

2003 - $6.8 trillion, 2004 - $7.4 trillion, 2005 - $7.9 trillion, 2006 - $8.5 trillion, 2007 - $9.0 trillion, 2008 - $10.0 trillion, 2009 - $11.9 trillion, 2010 - $13.5 trillion, 2011 - $14.8 trillion, 2012 - $16.1 trillion

Over the past several years, there has been a fair amount of discussion and debate as to whether there ought to be an amendment to the US Constitution to require a balance budget. While this might be somewhat helpful, our Editorial Board does not believe that such an amendment is necessary. Instead, what the country (desperately) needs is for our elected officials to simply re-structure (reduce) the magnitude of the federal government's spending, and implement a "more than balanced" budget. If the country were to be treated as a business enterprise, this entity would have been put on a financial institution's (ie, a bank's) "watch list" several years ago, and that bank would demand that the entity hire a turnaround consultant to get its financial house in order. The country did get such a wake-up call on August 5, 2011, when the credit rating agency Standard & Poor's lowered the country's credit rating to AA+ from AAA. Standard & Poor's issued a strongly worded critique of the American political system, saying that "political brinkmanship" over the debt had made the federal government's ability to manage its finances less stable, less effective and less predictable.

Our elected officials need to sharply curtail the magnitude of the federal government's spending, and then set a level of tax inflows that will be sufficient to create the surplus needed to begin repaying the $16.1 trillion cumulative debt over a reasonable period of time. We are proposing that an annual surplus of $1 trillion per year be generated, so that the cumulative US debt amount can be repaid by the year 2030 (or so).

Governmental (i.e., "Public") Pension Obligations

In our Conversation Piece entitled *Who is working for who?* our Editorial Board makes a number of recommendations on re-balancing and correcting (restoring) the relationship between private sector and public sector compensation. This re-balancing needs to be addressed and corrected in order to ensure the long term financial health of the country, and our federal and state governmental units.

Our Editorial Board believes that we have collectively gotten into our current sorry state of financial condition due to our elected officials' blatant mis-use of OPM (Other People's Money). In our other Conversation Pieces, we make specific recommendations on how to go about correcting these wrongs.

The purpose of this Conversation Piece is to first discuss the conceptual issues surrounding "employee benefits" in the private sector and in the governmental sector, and to make recommendation on how to move forward. We-the-People need to remember that our elected officials are our employees. They do not own their office - they are merely renting it for the Terms that we allow them to rent the position. Accordingly, we should deal with our elected officials in the same way that a private sector employer would deal with their employees – fairly and with mutual respect. It is unfortunate that our Editorial Board, if pressed, would feel compelled to characterize the current employment situation as one where the employer (We-the-People) have developed minimal respect for the employee (our elected officials). We need to get this fixed.

In order to help restore that mutual respect for our employees, We-the-People need to re-acquire that feeling that we are getting our money's worth. We need to re-address the compensation that we are paying to our employees, to ensure that the amount is appropriate. Our Editorial Board does not have any specific viewpoints or recommendations regarding the salaries paid to our elected "executive" or "legislative" employees. However, we do have a number of significant issues and concerns in regards to the fringe benefits, and we have some specific recommendations.

Our first concern is that federal government employees do not participate in the same health insurance programs utilized by the private sector. This "discrepancy" is one of the many sources of distrust and discontent with our elected employees and the bureaucracies that support our governmental functions. We don't really know why this situation was allowed to happen in the past, but going forward, with the passage of universal healthcare and the establishment of state healthcare exchanges, this disparity is the first discrepancy that should be eliminated. Any elected official who represents us in Washington DC should be covered through the state health insurance exchange of their home state. Federal government employees who live within the boundaries of Washington DC should be covered by a similar state health insurance exchange for Washington DC.

Our second (and more significant) concern is in regards to public sector pension benefits. As anyone in the private sector realizes, the defined benefit pension plan has generally been eliminated from the marketplace. This is primarily due to the downside problems associated with trying to maintain a properly funded corporate pension plan on behalf of the company's employees. Accordingly, private sector entities have moved the responsibility of providing for a financially secure retirement to the employees themselves thru a 401K savings plan or through personal IRAs. It is time for this evolution to also occur in the public sector.

Our Editorial Board does not believe that any elected official should receive a pension. They are merely renting their elective office. They should provide for their own retirement (by saving a portion of their compensation) just like employees in the private sector. Please note that we are not proposing that any past promises be rescinded – what we are proposing is that the new rules would be put into place for all newly elected officials who are seeking to rent their elective office in the future. To satisfy past promises, we recommend that the same procedures that are used in the private sector be utilized to quantify (and fund) all past promises (over a specified short period of time, if need be) to people who have been elected in the past, who were promised something under the old rules. Moving forward, the financial management of those (now personal) funds, and the financial risks associated with those funds, should be under the control of the people who earned those benefits in the past under the old rules. This will put these elected employees on the same footing as employees in the private sector. There should not be any new "pension" benefits for elected officials. Ever. Our viewpoint is that if an elected official has faithfully and effectively discharged the responsibilities of their office, they should have been able to establish the necessary credentials and networking contacts while in office, which should benefit them when they return to the private sector after their "rental period" has ended. This is, in effect, their "pension benefit" for their public service. They should not also own a permanent perpetual cash flow stream stemming from their years of public service. It is immoral to push the financial responsibility for such a cash flow stream on to future generations.

This is also our Editorial Board's primary discontent in regards to the public sector employees who are employed by the government bureaucracies. Employees in the private sector are being asked to take Personal Responsibility for their own financial requirements for their retirement years. It is time to level the playing field with the employees in the public sector.

Our Editorial Board is appalled by the horrendous financial condition of public sector pensions. Not only do we have funding problems with a number of federal pension plans, the problem is even worse at the state and local level. It appears that state and local politicians have learned (too well) the schemes associated with using Other People's Money, and pushing the financial responsibility for current promises on to future generations of citizens. On the internet are two reports about public pensions. The first is a survey of all 50 states, showing the best and worst run states in America. This report shows the amount of debt per capita, along with the state's budget deficit. Unfortunately, this is a somewhat misleading report, because (like the federal government and Social Security) the debt per capita does not includes the liability for public sector employee pension benefits that have not yet been appropriately funded. It is interesting to note that this type of accounting and financial management is not allowed in the private sector.

The second report is a similar report for major cities across the country. The amounts in this report are for unfunded pensions and retiree health plans. Local governmental units are just as guilty in regards to failing to adequately currently fund the promises being made to their governmental employees, including their police force and firefighters. This report by the Pew Charitable Trusts found that 61 US cities had a collective funding gap of more than $217 billion in future pension and healthcare obligations that they will owe to retiring workers in the future. The only way to prevent the improper use of Other People's Money is to put the Personal Responsibility for providing for their own financially secure retirement on to public sector employees, the same as for private sector employees.

The Political Process / Gridlock

The following is a recap of the current (sad) state of our country's political process. If you look at the level of voter participation in presidential election

years, compared to the "off year" elections (where the voting is for US
Senators and Congressional Representatives only) there has been a consistent
13 - 16 percentage point difference (decrease) in the level of voter participation
in the "off year" elections, where less than half of the voting-age population
bothers to go to the polls. However, the more alarming trend is that the
overall level of participation for both the "on year" and "off year" elections has
decreased by approximately 10 percentage points over the years -

Voting-age population		Voter turnout	Voter Turnout %
1960	109,159,000	68,838,204	63.1 %
1962	112,423,000	53,141,227	47.3
2010	235,809,266	90,682,968	37.8
2012	240,926,957	130,234,600	53.6

So.... What is contributing to the decrease in voter participation? By
definition, the decrease in voter turnout directly correlates to a corresponding
increase in voter apathy - - a sizeable portion of the electorate feels that their
vote won't make a difference in the country's direction, and "business as
usual" will therefore continue to be the norm in Washington DC, because the
country's political process is gridlocked and is not capable of moving forward.

Our Editorial Board feels differently. We believe that there are elected leaders
in both parties who share our concern about the state of our country's finances,
and who can work together to make the changes that are needed to Fix the
Debt. As we mentioned on our Home Page, the Foundation to Promote
Personal Responsibility is a national **non-partisan** organization that was
formed to do whatever we can, to put the country on a better fiscal path. We
don't care if our members are a Democrat, Republican, Libertarian,
Independent, or "etc". Our Foundation was created to support those
candidates who agree that it is immoral to push our country's fiscal problems
and debt onto future generations.

Term Limits and Campaign Finance Reform

As we have mentioned elsewhere on our website, our Editorial Board does not
believe that there are very many changes that need to be made to the "social
contract" between the federal government and its citizens (i.e., the US
Constitution) - - we believe the country's Founders did a pretty good job.
However, there are several references in the Federalist Papers (most notably in
Federalist Papers #s 41 and 57), where one of the major concerns was (and

continues to be) controlling the lust for power (by an individual and/or collectively for the government as a whole).

Even though there has always been this concern since Day 1, the Founders did not write specific Term Limits into the US Constitution. However, We-the-People did finally address this issue in regards to the Executive branch of the federal government (the President) via the 22nd Amendment, which was passed by Congress in 1947 and ratified in 1951 –

No person shall be elected to the office of the President more than twice, and no person who has held the office of President, or acted as President, for more than two years of a term to which some other person was elected President shall be elected to the office of President more than once.

Our Editorial Board believes that now is the time in our country's history, to extend this concept of Term Limits to the Legislative branch as well. It was never intended that a person should "permanently own" an elected position. This is borne out in the Federalist Papers. We also believe that one of the responsibilities of an elected official is to identify, educate and train their potential successor. We believe that the concept of Term Limits should be applied to the executive branch and all legislative branch positions at both the federal and state level. Although beyond the scope of what our Foundation intends to accomplish, we also believe that this concept of Term Limits (and the responsibility to identify, educate and train their potential successor) is appropriate at the local level as well.

Many people will argue that implementing Term Limits will discourage people from following their interests (and passion) in regards to public service. However, when you consider local executive branch and legislative branch positions, and state positions, and federal positions, there are plenty of opportunities for an individual to pursue their passion for public service. What we need to protect against is an individual's (sole) passion for power, and the potential passion for self-enrichment.

We also support the concept of one re-election for an elected position. This re-election could occur in the subsequent election or (if the person wants to take an intervening break) at some other point down the road in the future. In a way, this opportunity to run for re-election represents a way to help an elected official assess their degree of success in fulfilling the responsibility of the position, by asking the electorate to re-affirm their performance in the re-election process.

[Just as an aside, our Editorial Board is currently debating whether we should recommend that the US Supreme Court also be elected by We-the-People, and serve specified terms, with one potential re-election. We recognize that there are good and valid reasons why the judicial system was set up in the manner that it was established, to keep the interpretation of the country's laws separate from the political (election) process. Accordingly, we currently do not believe the member of the Court should be elected, by maybe the concept of Term Limits should be applied to the US Supreme Court. We are interested in hearing other viewpoints from our Foundation's members.]

Our Editorial Board is also discussing the issue of Campaign Finance reform. We appreciate the position of the Supreme Court in this arena - any attempt to regulate or set limits on the funding for the elections process is an infringement of the Freedom of Speech (i.e., money talks). However, we also believe that many of the rules that have been put into place over the years regarding the "fair" maximum amounts that an individual and/or group (PAC) may contribute are generally OK.

Campaign Finance is a highly complex "regulatory" issue, and we don't have any specific recommendations at this point in time, but we may be making some recommendations on Campaign Finance reform in the future, based on feedback from our Foundation's members.

The bottom line is that the "problem" with the election process is not so much the amount of money that is spent in the election process to "buy an office", but the problem is that the election process has a tendency to turn off a good portion (approximately half) of the electorate. Too much of the money raised can be spent on personal attack ads, rather than on addressing government policy issues and how a candidate's positions on the various issues can distinguish that candidate from their opponent. We're not saying that personal integrity issues aren't important (they can be vitally important), it's just that it is an unfortunate situation, that this aspect of the political process has a counter-effect of turning off the voting public.

"Don't Tread on Me" / There ought to be a law (or not)

"Don't Tread on Me" is one of our Editorial Board's favorite mottos. Its origin goes back to colonial times. In December 1775, Benjamin Franklin published an essay in the Pennsylvania Journal, in which he suggested that the rattlesnake was a good symbol for the American spirit. To paraphrase....
The rattlesnake is an emblem of vigilance – it never begins an attack, but once engaged, it does not surrender. The rattlesnake never wounds, until it has given appropriate notice to a potential enemy.

We feel that this sentiment continues to be very pertinent today in regards to a number of current issues facing the country - - the federal government's encroachment on personal liberties, the over-reach of the National Security Agency, and other examples where the executive or legislative branch have breached their constitutional limits.

Our Editorial Board's fundamental belief is that "less is more". We feel that many of the major political issues facing the country are caused by a bloated bureaucracy, and "entrenched" legislators who begin to feel that they need to propose additional laws to "solve a problem". This, in turn, contributes towards the ever-expanding reach of the federal government into people's daily lives. It also contributes to the phenomenon whereby the federal government, as a percent of GDP, has grown from 2.4% in 1887, to 7.9% in 1938, and to 25.2% in 2012. The final conundrum is that our elected officials do not seem to have the courage to ask the current generation of citizens to fund the programs that they have proposed and voted on to establish (setting aside the question as to whether the program was actually needed or not in the first place) because it is easier to push those obligations on to future generations.

So, the first question is.... Do we need the law / government program, or not. Our Editorial Board's default position is NOT.

The (New) Federalist Papers

As you may recall from your history books, The Federalist Papers were published in several newspapers during 1787 and 1788, with the intent to persuade voters to ratify the new proposed US Constitution. There were 85 essays written by Alexander Hamilton, James Madison and John Jay, which outlined how the new federal government would operate, along with the reasoning behind various sections of the proposed Constitution, and why this type of government was the best choice for the United States of America. We have provided a link to a website that provides further links to each of The Federalist Papers, in the event that you want to learn more about the background and reasoning on the various issues.

http://www.foundingfathers.info/federalistpapers/

As we have mentioned elsewhere on our website, one of the missions of our Editorial Board is to provide links to various sources of wisdom. We believe that the Founding Fathers had most of this pretty well laid out. However, over the years, we feel that in a number of key areas (primarily in regards to the expanding role of the government, versus a Personal Responsibility) our federal government has strayed away from the original game plan.

The purpose of this conversation piece is to highlight a few of the key thoughts that were written in The Federalist Papers regarding the new federal government –

No. 30 – Concerning the General Power of Taxation.... *It has been already observed that the federal government ought to possess the power of providing for the support of the national forces; in which proposition was intended to be included the expense of raising troops, of building and equipping fleets, and all other expenses in any wise connected with military arrangements and operations.*

No. 41 – General View of the Powers Conferred by The Constitution... *...two important questions arise: 1. Whether any part of the powers transferred to the general government be unnecessary or improper? 2. Whether the entire mass of them be dangerous to the portion of jurisdiction left in the several States?*

... in every political institution, a power to advance the public happiness involves a discretion which may be misapplied and abused. .... in all cases where power is to be conferred, the point first to be decided is, whether such a power be necessary to the public good; as the next will be, in case of an affirmative decision, to guard as effectually as possible against a perversion of the power to the public detriment.

That we may form a correct judgment on this subject, it will be proper to review the several powers conferred on the government.... 1. Security against foreign danger; 2. Regulation of the intercourse with foreign nations; 3. Maintenance of harmony and proper intercourse among the States; 4. Certain miscellaneous objects of general utility; 5. Restraint of the States from certain injurious acts; 6. Provisions for giving due efficacy to all these powers.

No. 57 – The Alleged Tendency of the New Plan to Elevate the Few at the Expense of the Many Considered in Connection with Representation.... *The aim of every political constitution is, or ought to be, first to obtain for rulers men who possess most wisdom to discern, and most virtue to pursue, the common good of the society; and in the next place, to take the most effectual precautions for keeping them virtuous whilst they continue to hold their public trust... The means relied on in this form of government for preventing their degeneracy are numerous and various. The most effectual one is such a limitation of the term of appointments as will maintain a proper responsibility to the people.*

As we have noted elsewhere, one of our Editorial Board's objectives is to solicit additional ideas on good policies that should be implemented in the future. The key objective of our Join the Conversation section of the website is to have our Members contribute towards the writing of the New Federalist Papers of 2013-2014.

Capitalism, Communism and "Socialism"

Capitalism and Communism – pretty much opposite ends of the spectrum when it comes to the philosophical differences regarding how a country and its citizens should conduct their economic lives. Setting aside the governmental / political issues, and focusing solely on the economics, the essence of the difference relates to the ownership and control over the means of production. Under communism, everything is owned by the state. There is scant consideration given to the idea of an individual having the opportunity to assume Personal Responsibility for pursuing their own dreams and controlling their own fate. The communist system's societal philosophy is - *From each according to his ability, to each according to his needs.* So.... What marketplace assessment is available within that type of society to help assess each person's "abilities", and what kind of "entity" could possibly be intelligent enough that it can deliver to each specific person, what is needed to fulfill that person's hopes and aspirations, and satisfies that individual's specific interests and wants (i.e, beyond their basic day-to-day living "needs"- however defined)?

So, Communism – how has that been working out? You only need to review the results of history to assess the success of the communist system - - consider the ultimate fate of the Union of Soviet Socialist Republics (USSR), East Germany, North Korea, China, etc. The results are in. The USSR collapsed, East Germany re-unified with West Germany and is now more prosperous, North Korea continues to be a basket case, and China has abandoned the primary tenets of communism and is moving towards implementing market based economic policies (but of course, there is still the problem with basic personal freedoms and the one-party political system).

On the opposite end of the spectrum, the knock against capitalism is that it is a system where the major share of profits from the business will go to the owners of the business, while the employees of the business will get a smaller share. This "inequity" is what the supporters of communism would dearly love to eliminate. That is why communists feel that the ownership of the means of production should reside with the people / "the state". They fail to accept that the owners' profits represent a return on the owners' investment, and represents compensation for their investment risk.

The other major philosophical difference is in regards to individual freedoms. Communism asks each person to put the society before the individual, whereas capitalism puts individual freedoms (choices and Personal Responsibility) before society. Therefore, a second major knock against capitalism is that it plants the seeds of exploitation, where too much wealth and power is concentrated in the hands of a few people. However, from an innovation standpoint, nearly all of the greatest advances in human history (starting with fire and the wheel) have been due to individual creativity and enterprise. In today's world, capitalism (coupled with patents, trademarks and copyrights) protects the fruits of that creativity and enterprise. Communism, on the other hand, is not a system that nurtures creative aspirations.

So, if capitalism puts too much wealth and power in the hands of a few people, this is where "socialism" steps in. Socialism simply means that some level of societal / governmental regulation is needed. Another knock against capitalism is that it contributes towards class distinction – "haves" and "have-nots" / rich and poor. Socialism is a means to "narrow the multiples" between the rich and poor. In order to minimize the downside effects of class distinctions, the "bell curve" for a healthy capitalist system is a preponderance of the citizenry safely within the bounds of the "middle class", with the fringe portions of the bell curve being people living below the poverty level on one end of the spectrum, and a small wealthy elite on the other end (who have earned their right to live out there on that fringe).

Our Editorial Board's definition of "Useful Socialism" is trying to craft the best "tax math" to achieve the best bell curve. No one wants to live below the federal government's official poverty guideline level. Every individual's self-interest is best served by assuming Personal Responsibility to do what is necessary to improve their personal marketability, so that they can rise above the minimum wage. (The federal minimum wage should be part of the math for setting the official federal poverty guideline amount). In our conversation piece on *Tax Reform / Tax Simplification* we put forth our recommendation on the best math that should be used to accomplish "Useful Socialism". We are hopeful, that in the short term, the top marginal tax rate can be set no higher than 49%, and this rate could then be reduced in the future, once the cumulative US debt is repaid.

41

So.... What about federal estate taxes? Should babies be "born with a silver spoon in their mouth"? Yes - - to some degree. Is this amount "open ended"? Probably not. The "rights of the privileged" will always be a source of contention between the "have nots" and "haves". The beauty of our country (the land of opportunity) is that each person controls their own fate in regards to the possibility of becoming a "have".

So... Should some babies get a head start? We don't see how we can possibly answer this question other than by saying "unfortunately/fortunately yes". Should a person be able to pass on the fruits of their labors to their heirs? Absolutely. What is the right amount? We suspect that it's probably somewhat "OK as is". There isn't a right answer or a wrong answer, and you can get different viewpoints from talking to different people. The one thing that the country should not repeat is having the taxable estate amount bouncing around like it did during the past few years. And we shouldn't create a tax environment where people should be trying to time the year in which they should die.....

Liberalism and Conservatism

Liberal / Conservative - - In what regard? Our Editorial Board feels that we need to talk about both fiscal (monetary) issues and social issues.

Monetary issues are pretty straight forward. Conservatives support living within your means and spending less rather than more, and generally have an aversion to incurring debt. Liberals are more liberal in regards to cash outflows, and are more liberal in regards to the use of Other People's Money. Liberals are more supportive of higher taxes and bigger government. Accordingly, liberals believe in "free" universal healthcare, which should be provided "by the government" to all citizens. The government should also provide cash welfare payments and other government services to the less fortunate, and either increase the level of taxes to fund these governmental programs, or borrow from the future. But enough said.... Otherwise, we will start repeating ourselves (yet again).

So.... What about social issues? Liberals support a more expansive government, and accordingly, a bigger role for the government in people's lives. Conservatives prefer smaller government, less regulation, and prefer to see social services delivered by the private sector and/or Not-for-Profit organizations.

Conservatives rely upon a literal interpretation of the US Constitution, support the Bill of Rights, and support the concept of Personal Responsibility, and the reliance upon the private sector, rather than governmental programs. They support laws that reflect what they feel are the best interests of society as a whole - financially and morally.

Liberals support more government regulation and restrictions on certain rights, such as the right to bear arms, and are more liberal in regards to other social issues such as gay marriage, abortion and embryonic stem cell research.

One last distinction – conservatives believe that the states should have more power and independence, rather than relying upon the federal government. Liberals prefer a larger role for government – whether it be at the federal, state or local level.

Conservatives, Liberals and Libertarians –
And let's not forget the libertarians (who should not be confused with liberals). Libertarians believe that the role of government should be extremely limited in both the economic and social spheres. On economic issues, libertarians believe in the private sector and the free market rather than government bureaucracies (the private sector and marketplace make better decisions on resource allocation). On social issues, the primary focus of libertarians is the maximization of civil liberties for all citizens. An appropriate motto for libertarians is "Don't tread on me".

Our Editorial Board believes that in regards to fiscal issues (and the size of the federal and state governments) "less is better". In cases where there is a necessary government program, those programs should be moved from the federal level to the state level as much as possible. On social issues, we support minimal (rather than "liberal" doses of) governmental intrusion into people's personal lives.

The Declaration of Independence - Taxation without representation / Taxation with representation

We hold these truths to be self-evident – all men are created equal, and they have unalienable rights to life, liberty and the pursuit of happiness. Pretty profound, and yet pretty simple and straightforward, too.

Governments are instituted among men, deriving powers from the consent of the governed. Whenever any form of government becomes destructive to those ends, it is the right of the people to alter it. We agree.

The history of the present King of Great Britain is a history of repeated injuries and usurpations. The Declaration of Independence went on to list each of the colonies' grievances, which included – *For imposing taxes on us without our consent. For abolishing our most valuable laws, and altering fundamentally the forms of our governments. For suspending our own legislatures, and declaring themselves invested with power to legislate for us in all cases whatsoever.*

The passages above pretty much summarize the grievance commonly referred to as "taxation without representation". So, what do our current public opinion polls indicate about how today's citizens feel about the current state of our government(s)? Those polls indicate that the population is not very pleased with the current approach towards "taxation *with* representation".

Setting aside the poll results - how effective is our current representative form of government, and how effective is the citizenry's oversight of those legislative functions? Unfortunately, it's not very good. The feeling is that we have created an entrenched legislature that is taxing the population fairly heavily, but at the same time is spending even more than what the government is taking in.

Our Editorial Board supports taking whatever steps are needed to reduce the size of the federal government, and collect the tax revenues that are needed to begin paying down the US debt over a reasonable period of time. We also need to make sure that we have an effective legislative branch and an effective executive branch that will fulfill their "checks and balances" responsibilities, to ensure that we do not begin repeating these same mistakes in the future.

The US Constitution and The Bill of Rights

We the People of the United States, in order to form a more perfect union.... wrote and approved a pretty good US Constitution. It has successfully stood the test of time. In the beginning, there was a lot of debate about whether the document was comprehensive enough, and so We-the-People filled in the blanks with the Bill of Rights, and the first ten amendments were ratified on December 15, 1791.

One of the beautiful things about the US Constitution is that it is can be updated, whenever We-the-People deem it necessary to do so. To date there have been twenty-seven amendments (twenty-five when you consider the fact that the country implemented Prohibition with the 18th Amendment, and then repealed it fourteen years later with the 21st Amendment).

As we have noted elsewhere, our Editorial Board does not feel that there are any major changes that need to be made to the current "social contract", except for Term Limits. We recommend that We-the-People apply the wisdom embedded within the 22nd amendment (regarding Term Limits for the US President), and follow the same logic and reasoning in regards to all of our elected officials in the legislative branch (our Senators and Congressional representatives). We also believe that these Term Limit concepts should be applicable to all executive and legislative positions at the state level as well.

1984 in 2013

The 1st Amendment to the US Constitution guarantees the freedom of speech. Although Eric Blair (whose pen name was George Orwell) was a British citizen, he was fortunate to live in a similarly free society that gave him the freedom to express his views of the world (and also convey his warnings about the potential for abuses that could be committed by a totalitarian / authoritarian government) in his most noteworthy work of fiction..... (Or was it?)

In his book *Nineteen Eighty-Four*, George Orwell wrote about a government headed by Big Brother and The Party, who justified their rule in the name of the supposed greater good. The inhabitants of Oceania had no real privacy. Many of the citizens lived in apartments equipped with two-way telescreens, so that they could be watched and listened to at any time. The Thought Police, whose role was to suppress all dissenting opinion, would employ undercover agents who posed as normal citizens and reported any person with subversive tendencies. A major theme of the book was censorship and the role of the Ministry of Truth, where photographs were doctored and public archives were continually rewritten.

The adjective *Orwellian* has come to describe official deception, secret surveillance, and manipulation of the citizenry by a totalitarian / authoritarian state.

In November 2011, the federal government argued before the US Supreme Court that it wanted to continue to utilize GPS tracking of individuals without first seeking a warrant. Supreme Court Justice Stephen Breyer questioned what that meant for a democratic society by asking, "If you win this case, then there is nothing to prevent the police or the government from monitoring 24-hours a day the public movement of every citizen of the United States. So if you win, you suddenly produce what sounds like *Nineteen Eighty-Four*."

The members of Our Editorial Board are not conspiracy theorists, and most of us are not paranoid. ☺ We are providing this Conversation Piece to not only pay homage to George Orwell's work of fiction, but also to emphasize the wisdom of (and the absolute importance of) our Founders' Fourth Amendment (from back in 1789) –

The right of the people to be secure in their persons, houses, papers, and effects, against unreasonable searches and seizures, shall not be violated, and no Warrants shall issue, but upon probable cause, supported by Oath or affirmation, and particularly describing the place to be searched, and the persons or things to be seized.

Simply put – "generic" monitoring of the entire population should not be allowed. Searches and seizures should only occur after the issuance of a warrant, after establishing "probable cause."

Welfare Reform

Our Editorial Board's recommendation for welfare reform calls for the elimination of all federal and state cash welfare payments to an individual. OK - a lot of readers will be shocked and deplored by that statement, and their reaction will be "....*those heartless S.O.B.s*...." However, nothing could be further from the truth. We only want to get the federal and state governments out of the business of dispensing cash welfare payments to individuals.

The democracy will cease to exist when you take away from those who are willing to work and give to those who would not. ...Thomas Jefferson

We share Thomas Jefferson's concern that a society is at risk, when its citizens can easily obtain cash benefits from their government. The recipients will begin to rationalize that those payments represent an entitlement, and they will begin to rely upon that government welfare program, rather than take Personal Responsibility for bettering their own personal lives.

So, does that mean We-the-People should ignore the daily struggles of those citizens who live below the applicable federal poverty guideline amount, and who struggle to meet their daily living needs? Absolutely not. As we discuss in the Conversation Piece **entitled *What the Federal Government Should (and Should Not) Do***, we make the case that the best vehicle(s) for delivering "social services" (and "welfare") to an individual (and if necessary, to that individual's family) are religious organizations and Not-for-Profit organizations. And as we discuss in the Conversation Piece entitled *Tax Reform / Tax Simplification*, we make a recommendation that the federal government can support these religious and charitable organizations via the country's federal income tax policies.

What about unemployment benefits? We believe that the federal government and state governments should continue to collect this type of payroll tax revenues from employers. However, the federal government should immediately fund those payments back to the applicable state. And as we mentioned above, we believe that state governments should not provide cash welfare payments to its citizens. Instead, these unemployment tax receipts should be distributed by the state to the appropriate Not-for-Profit organizations that the state's citizens should look to for assistance – whether it be a state or local food bank, a local Habitat for Humanity type of entity, an entity that can provide assistance in paying utility costs, or an organization that provides remedial job skills re-training, etc.

Our Editorial Board is also gravely concerned about the state of the family in today's society. The number of single parent households is alarming, as this represents a much more challenging situation for that family unit, when one of the parents is not present in a child's daily life. Facing the challenges of day to day life is much easier with the support of a strong family unit, and is easier still when there is a strong extended family that includes grandparents, aunts, uncles and cousins. We believe that a strong family unit is needed to nurture our society's children, as they begin to take on the Personal Responsibility for their own lives.

The Foundation's Agenda

As we have mentioned elsewhere on our website, we believe in the principles that were put forth by our country's Founders, and are appreciative of the resulting solid foundation that our Founders built for our society. However, We-the-People have strayed away from some of those core principles, and therefore we face an urgent and profound issue in regards to the size and growth and spending of the federal government, and the resulting cumulative US debt. However, we believe that these problems can be successfully rectified by re-structuring the role and the scope the federal government, by pushing the responsibilities for daily living away from federal government programs and more in the direction of individual Personal Responsibility.

Our Foundation's agenda is educational – we disseminate facts.

Our agenda also includes putting forth recommendations on how the country can move forward, in order to solve the annual deficit and begin repaying the cumulative US debt.

Our agenda includes soliciting additional perspectives and other recommendations (and other people's wisdom) from our Foundation's members.

We intend to approach our currently elected government representatives, at both the federal and state levels, to garner their support in implementing these recommended changes.

We also intend to support those candidates for public office (at both the federal and state levels) who support the Foundation's recommendations, and who will legislate for the passage and implementation of these initiatives.

A Letter to Senator Bernie Sanders regarding Social Security

July 5, 2015

Dear Senator Sanders,

I have been reading a number of recent newspaper articles that mention you believe the federal government should increase the amount of Social Security benefits that are being paid to our country's citizens. However, this is money that the country doesn't have, because the federal government is already in debt by over $18 trillion.

I have run five scenarios through the benefits calculator on the Social Security website to see the relationships between Lifetime Wages, Payroll Tax Withholdings, and the resulting Social Security benefits. All five scenarios are similar in that the person starts receiving wages at age 19, they work for 47 years, retire at age 66 (the normal retirement age), and then receive benefits for 19 years until the end of a life expectancy of age 85.

The five scenarios are - - 1. a "Barely Eligible" recipient, 2. a "Minimum Wage" recipient, 3. a "Middle Class" recipient (50% of the Social Security wage cap), 4. an "Upper Middle Class" recipient (100% of the wage cap), and 5. a "Very Well Off" recipient (two times the wage cap).

I have attached schedules that show the amounts for each of these five scenarios, but the summary is as follows –

	Lifetime wages	SS Withheld	SS Benefits *	Multiple	Amt over
# 1	$ 48,837	$ 3,028	$ 25,536	8.4	$ 22,508
# 2	$ 415,022	$ 25,731	$ 226,176	8.8	$ 200,445
# 3	$ 1,355,650	$ 84,050	$ 440,040	5.2	$ 355,990
# 4	$ 2,711,300	$ 168,101	$ 601,692	3.6	$ 433,591
# 5	$ 5,422,600	$ 168,101	$ 601,692	3.6	$ 433,591

* The total benefits received exclude any future Cost of Living Allowance increases

Also, please keep in mind that people do not need to work 47 years (or earn these wage amounts) to qualify for the benefit amounts shown above, so the real "Multiple(s)" are usually higher.

I have the following Questions / Observations –

Re: Scenario # 1 – I would think that if there is a citizen who probably needs to receive a "social security" payment, it would be the person in Scenario #1. Shouldn't Social Security be changed so that it provides (to someone who qualifies for welfare) a benefit amount that is at least equal to the federal poverty guideline amount?

Re: Scenario # 2 – The person who makes the minimum wage for 47 years receives an annual Social Security benefit of $11,904, which is $134 over the federal poverty guideline amount. Maybe this scenario is OK.

Re: Scenario # 3 – I believe the reason that 8 out of 10 people think Social Security is such a great program is that many of our country's citizens get back more than five times the amount they paid into the program. However, another way to look at Social Security is that our country's citizens are being bribed with our money. What is even worse is that (in reality) it is our children's and grandchildren's money.

Re: Scenarios # 4 and 5 – What is the purpose of this government program that pays out these "unfunded pension benefits" to people who don't really need to receive these payments? Why should the federal government pay "financially secure" people $433,591 more than they paid into Social Security?

In President Obama's latest budget, the amount of the 2015 deficit that is attributed to Social Security is $125 billion (outflows of $891 billion vs. tax receipts of $766 billion). This annual deficit amount is expected to increase to $361 billion in 2025 (outflows of $1.569 trillion vs. tax receipts of $1.208 trillion).

I realize that things were different back in 1935 during the Great Depression when Social Security was established. But in today's world (with fewer than three workers for every retiree and with an increase in life expectancy) the benefits that are being paid out under the existing Social Security program are upside down, make no sense, and are unsustainable. Social Security certainly shouldn't be enhanced. Instead it should be transformed into a means-tested welfare program. All current retirees / recipients should be "grandfathered" under the existing rules, however, eventually all monthly "pension payments" should be phased out by the end of the transition period. Social security should be transformed into a welfare benefit – an amount that should only be paid to elderly retirees who need financial assistance. Otherwise, this program will continue to steal huge sums of money from our children and grandchildren.

Sincerely yours,

Tim Beck

Attachments

The 2020 Initiative

The six planks of The 2020 Initiative are as follows –

1 – Re-establish fiscal responsibility -

The growing US debt problem represents a complete and unequivocal failure of our country's leadership (both the executive and the legislative branches) on a scale that is unprecedented in our country's history. The $20 trillion of "on book" debt (an amount in excess of $61,000 for every man, woman, child and retiree in the country) is **unacceptable**. Every child that is born in our country comes into this world with a $61,000 debt hanging over their head, caused by the mismanagement of our federal government's operations by our elected officials. It is time to completely overhaul and restructure the federal government's finances. We need to eliminate deficit spending and begin to repay the cumulative US debt.

2 – Implement Term Limits for members of the US Senate and US House of Representatives –

We need to pass the proposed constitutional amendment (see www.termlimits.org).

3 – Scrap and re-write the entire federal income tax code for personal income tax returns –

The current federal income tax code for personal income tax returns needs to be completely rewritten and simplified. The tax code has become nearly incomprehensible to the average citizen, and contains too many provisions that dole out favoritism to "special interest groups". The changes to the personal income tax code must be accompanied by corresponding changes regarding welfare reform, the transformation of the country's Social Security program, and the reform of the country's Medical Care taxes (see below).

4 – Welfare Reform –

The real solution to the problem of poverty is to help those less fortunate become "unpoor". The federal government and its current welfare programs cannot accomplish this task. The real solution is for the federal government to eliminate all of its welfare programs, and instead support civil society (families, who are supported by Not-for-Profit charities and religious organizations) to help people take Personal Responsibility for their own lives.

Financial support to these Not-for-Profit charitable organizations will be provided via changes to the federal income tax code.

5 – Reform / Transform Social Security over a multi-year transition period –

The original intent of the Social Security program was to provide a safety net (welfare) to keep the elderly out of poverty. However, the Social Security program that was set up provides an "entitlement" to all citizens, without regard to a person's / family's financial needs during retirement. This is the fundamental flaw in the program that was established in 1935. Current demographics along with projections of upcoming changes to the population continue to foreshadow a complete breakdown of the current system. Social Security must be fundamentally transformed over a multi-year transition period.

6 – Reform the US Healthcare system –

The federal government must be removed from the administration of the country's healthcare system. Medicare must also be fundamentally transformed. To serve the people who have not yet retired, the healthcare system must be returned to the private sector, and it must be managed at the state and local level. The federal bureaucracies that have a current role in the country's healthcare system must be transformed from being a provider / administrator / payor, and instead become a consultative resource to the states and local agencies (including Not-for-Profit charitable organizations) that will have the responsibility for delivering healthcare services to our country's citizens. The Department of Health and Human Services (with approval by the US House of Representatives and US Senate) will have the responsibility to set the minimum federal healthcare requirements for the "bronze level national standard" to be offered within each state, for those people who want to elect that level of coverage and the "public" option.

The Principles underlying The 2020 Initiative are as follows –

1 - Re-establish Fiscal Responsibility at the federal level -

It is immoral for the federal government to push a constantly growing debt problem onto future generations.

The federal government must live within its means, just the same as any individual, family, or business enterprise is expected to do. The federal government is NOT any different in regards to the need to maintain fiscal responsibility.

It is unsound fiscal policy for the government to promise something (or commit to something) within the current time frame, and then defer the financial obligation for that program to the future.

2 - Implement Term Limits for members of the US Senate and US House of Representatives –

With the current congressional approval rating in the low teens (and which has not shown any improvement over the past several years) it is time for our elected officials to work with our country's citizens to change the rules regarding Term Limits for members of the US Senate and US House of Representatives.

It is time to implement Term Limits, so that our elected legislators can make decisions that advance the cause(s) of the country as a whole, rather than make decisions that are affected by their concerns about their long-term political career. It is time for our elected officials to go ahead and "touch the third rail of politics" and reform our country's "entitlement" programs.

Power corrupts and absolute power corrupts absolutely. George Washington was adamantly opposed to the idea of an "imperial presidency" and vowed to serve at most two terms. We need to extend the wisdom of the 22nd Amendment and apply it to the US Senate and US House of

Representatives as well. The intent of the US Constitution was to have a government run by We-the-People, not by entrenched career politicians who are beholden to special interest groups.

Imagine what would happen if members of Congress knew that from Day 1, they had been elected to get a job done, and had only a limited amount of time to perform their service and make a difference. No longer would this be a "career", but it would represent an opportunity to serve their country, as the Founders envisioned.

3 - Scrap and re-write the entire federal income tax code for personal income tax returns –

Our country's tax code must be simple and easily understood by our country's citizens.

The tax system should simply raise revenue for the government - - it should not be used to "socially engineer" our country's citizens.

Government should not use the tax code to intrude upon the private sector / the marketplace.

The tax system must produce an amount of revenue that equals / exceeds the cost of government.

4 - Welfare Reform –

Until an individual / family is able to take complete Personal Responsibility for their own lives, there will continue to be a need for welfare assistance.

Eligibility for welfare assistance should be determined annually based upon an individual's / family's financial situation - - their annual income and accumulated wealth (i.e., "means tested").

Beginning in 2020, there should no longer be any federal cash welfare payments to individuals. (It is recommended that there should also not be any state-provided cash welfare payments).

The goods and services that welfare-eligible recipients need to receive should be provided by Not-for-Profit charitable organizations, not via government welfare programs.

One of the primary priorities of welfare assistance should be in regards to education services, including remedial education assistance and job re-training, in order to help people obtain meaningful employment (above the minimum wage).

5 - Reform / Transform Social Security over a multi-year transition period –

The responsibility to provide for one's own financial security during retirement is a Personal Responsibility. It is not an appropriate role of the federal government.

The deferral of a taxpayer's taxable income via Individual Retirement Accounts, 401(k) plans, etc. should continue to be a key feature of the federal income tax code.

It is OK for the federal government to provide a welfare benefit to an elderly citizen who requires such financial assistance.

6 - Reform the US Healthcare system –

The responsibility to provide for one's own medical costs is a Personal Responsibility. It is not an appropriate role of the federal government.

The government should make available to every citizen the opportunity to establish a Health Savings Account, including those situations where an HSA plan is not available via an individual's employer.

It is OK for the federal government to establish the minimum healthcare benefits that should be available to all of our country's citizens, and to protect our citizens' rights in regards to these minimum coverages.

Discussion Points and Recommendations –

1 - Re-establish Fiscal Responsibility at the federal level –

We need to have our elected officials acknowledge that the growing cumulative debt amount is a problem that threatens our country's future. We need our elected officials to commit to solving the growing debt problem, now.

We need to limit the federal government's role to its two primary purposes (only) - - to protect individuals' rights that have been granted under the US Constitution, and to militarily protect the country as a whole.

The President must be given the power of the Line Item Veto. If so exercised, any line item veto could subsequently be over-ridden by the citizens' representatives with a two-thirds vote in both the US House and US Senate.

The federal government is responsible for the protection and general welfare of the country (collectively as a whole).

No governmental unit at any level is responsible for the financial welfare of an individual - - this is a Personal Responsibility of each individual and their family.

If necessary, assistance will be made available to that individual / family from Not-for-Profit charitable organizations.

2 - Implement Term Limits for members of the US Senate and US House of Representatives –

The proposed amendment to the US Constitution (see www.termlimits.org) calls for a two-term limit on members of the US Senate (a maximum of 12 years) and a three-term limit on members of the US House of Representatives (a maximum of 6 years).

According to recent polls, more than 70% of US citizens support the concept of implementing Term Limits for members of the US Senate and US House of Representatives. It is time to implement this change.

Campaign finance restrictions are illegal per the US Supreme Court. In addition, corporations are allowed to fund (make contributions to) political campaigns. Money influences elections, and those funds are being invested by individuals and special interest groups for their own special interest.

More than 70% of US citizens believe that current election rules (and campaign finance advantages) favor incumbents.

Term Limits fortify democracy by expanding voter choice and the competition for voters' votes.

Setting a limit on the number of years an elected official can hold a particular office will serve to advance two primary objectives. Term Limits will serve to increase the "cost of capital" for the various special interest groups, because such groups' "investment" will need to be recovered over a shorter period of time (rather than in perpetuity) and this will serve to dampen the effectiveness of the money that is injected into the political process. And more importantly, Term Limits will result in new candidates each election cycle, who will bring new thoughts and ideas to the US Senate and US House of Representatives.

With its ever-expanding role and power, the federal government has begun to encroach upon the citizens' civil liberties (something that our country's Founders warned against).

One of the other primary concerns at the time the US Constitution was approved was to guard against the possible self-aggrandizement of our elected officials. Today we find many government programs and policies that have served to create a separate class distinction between the citizenry (the governed) and our elected officials.

The original intent was to have a constant flow of citizens into and out of public life - - elected officials who would run for office to provide public service to their fellow citizens, rather than for their own personal gain.

Therefore, we also need to begin to remove all distinctions that have arisen between people in public life (the government) vs. private citizens. We need to eliminate separate healthcare programs for elected officials and government employees.

We also need to eliminate public pensions for people who are elected to office. Public pensions are not necessary (or appropriate) for people who are elected to public office. If the person is effective and successful in being an elected official, they will be able to subsequently leverage that experience in any future endeavors they would want to pursue once they leave office. Pensions upon leaving office are not appropriate, and therefore, no additional ongoing (lifetime) cash should be paid to that individual.

During their term(s) in office, elected officials should be entitled to make personal contributions to an IRA / 401(k) plan, similar to citizens in the private sector. [Note: We recognize that there will need to be a transition plan for people who have currently been promised a pension, to move from the current arrangements to new rules regarding the elimination of all public pensions.]

For employees in the federal public sector, we need to begin to transition all retirement programs from a pension plan to a defined contribution retirement program (i.e., a 401K plan) to match what is happening in the private sector.

The only appropriate pensions that the federal government should pay are to personnel who served in our country's armed forces for a minimum of ten years, or who were wounded during their service to our country. These pension programs for military personnel need to be funded each year (i.e, currently) using the same, sound pension funding rules that are required in the private sector.

Any unit of government (whether it be federal, state, or local) should be required to fund currently any public pension benefits that have been promised. It is immoral to push the cost of unfunded public pensions onto future generations. Unfunded public pensions are a major source of fiscal irresponsibility at the federal level (i.e., Social Security), state level (Illinois, Connecticut, California, etc.) and municipal level (Detroit, Chicago, New York, etc.).

3 - Scrap and re-write the federal income tax code for personal income tax returns –

The current federal income tax code for personal income tax returns needs to be completely rewritten and simplified. It is too complex and has become nearly incomprehensible (especially in regards to the new provisions for the Affordable Care Act).

The tax code is burdened with special deals and special provisions that only serve to promote the agenda(s) of the applicable special interest group(s). These special provisions serve to create effects that distort the marketplace.

All itemized deductions (mortgage interest, real estate taxes, charitable contributions, etc.) should be eliminated from the process of calculating taxable income. Instead, we should use an appropriate federal poverty guideline amount in the calculation of taxable income.

Poverty guideline amounts should be reviewed and set by Congress each year, and should cover the minimum basic essentials - the cost of food, housing, and medical care costs for various family sizes.

We should maintain the IRA / 401K deferral of income for personal retirement accounts (a Personal Responsibility).

We should expand the use of Health Savings Accounts to cover medical expenses that are not covered under a health insurance policy (a Personal Responsibility). Individuals should be allowed to set up a private HSA, in the event that such a plan is not available through their employer.

The compensation value of employer-provided health insurance should be included in W-2 wage income (see below regarding healthcare reform).

The following are our recommendations for tax reform –

We need to ensure a 100% accounting of all citizens for income tax purposes each year (see below regarding welfare reform). The IRS should perform a 100% reconciliation with the list of citizens maintained by the Social Security Administration, and identify any mismatches. IRS agents, Homeland Security agents and/or Social Security employees should follow up as necessary. "E-verify" is a key component of this cross-checking process.

This annually updated federal database of all people within our borders will be used by the IRS, the Social Security Administration, the Department of Homeland Security, and the US Census Bureau, and will include the following data fields (only) - Name, Social Security Number, Date of Birth, and Current Address.

The database should also contain "previously changed from" data for Prior Name and Prior Address (if applicable), to help the government track those changes from the prior year.

We should use IRS Form 1040 to serve as the definition of the family unit (or individual) for that year's taxes, and also have the 1040 Form serve as the source document to establish eligibility for welfare during the following year.

All families / individuals should be taxed a minimum of 10% of their wage income (via Social Security and Medical Care payroll tax withholdings).

Progressive income tax rates for incrementally higher levels of income above the federal poverty guideline amount are appropriate.

Taxable income ranges and the associated marginal income tax rates should be reviewed and adjusted annually, and be specifically approved by the US House of Representatives and US Senate each year in connection with the preparation of the annual budget.

Taxpayers would satisfy their annual federal income tax obligation via - 1) payroll tax withholdings (the sum of Social Security and Medical Care payroll tax withholdings and Federal income tax withholdings), 2) quarterly installment payments (as is done currently), 3) with qualifying Charitable Contribution offsets, and 4) with the remaining obligation to be paid to the US Treasury by April 15th.

No tax refund should ever be sent to a taxpayer until all income amounts, tax withholdings, installment tax payments, and charitable contribution offsets have been verified by the IRS' data matching systems, but no later than by May 31st.

Social Security and Medical Care payroll taxes should be paid on the entire amount of W-2 wage income. However, W-2 wage income should only be taxed once, and therefore these payroll tax withholdings are simply one component of an individual's / family's federal tax obligation.

Incremental federal income taxes would only be paid on income that is over and above the amount needed for basic survival (the federal poverty guideline amount).

There should not be any distinctions made regarding the taxation of income based on the nature of the income, whether it be from wages, net business income, pensions, social security benefits, interest, dividends, capital gains, etc.

Welfare benefits that have been received in the form of goods or services should be excluded from taxable income (as is done currently).

Any and all income earned over and above the amount that is needed for basic survival (the federal poverty guideline amount) should be subject to progressive tax rates, starting at a rate of 10%.

Progressive income tax rates are appropriate. For additional income that an individual / family makes over and above the federal poverty guideline amount, it is appropriate that each incremental level of income be subjected to a relatively higher marginal tax rate, until the cumulative US debt amount has been repaid.

The following taxable income ranges and associated marginal income tax rates should be established for 2020 –

For income levels below the federal poverty guideline amount, taxable income would be equal to $0 and there would be no incremental federal income taxes due. However, all W-2 wage income will be subject to Social Security taxes of 6.5% and Medical Care taxes of 3.5%.

For taxable incomes above the applicable federal poverty guideline amount, the following ranges and rates should be used, beginning in 2020: $0 to $25,000 - 10% / $25,000 to $100,000 - 20% / $100,000 to $250,000 - 30% / $250,000 to $1,000,000 - 40% / Over $1,000,000 - 45%

Starting in 2020, payroll tax withholdings that are paid to satisfy the intergenerational social responsibility for Social Security and Medicare would also be used to satisfy a portion of that individual's / family's federal income tax obligation for that year. Therefore, if an individual / family had $20,000 of W-2 wage income and $1,000 of other taxable income, they would pay the following taxes – - Social Security - $1,300, Medical Care - $700, and federal income taxes - $100.

Starting in 2020, the incremental 3.8% tax on investment income that was implemented to help fund Medicare would be eliminated. The .9% Additional Medicare tax would also be eliminated.

The maximum total of income taxes paid to the federal government should never exceed 45%. Beyond that point (when you consider state and local taxes), a person begins working for the government, rather than for their family.

The entire structure of taxable income ranges and associated income tax rates should be re-visited each year in the future, in connection with the annual federal budget process (and then lowered as appropriate) but only after we begin to repay the cumulative US debt amount.

Tax rates should never be lowered as long as there is an existing outstanding US debt amount.

In the near term, and in connection with the spending reductions outlined for Social Security and Medicare/Medicaid, and while the country's welfare policies are being transformed, and while we begin to repay the cumulative US debt amount, the highest marginal tax rate will be increased from 39.6% to 45%. This increase in the top marginal tax rate should be used exclusively to begin repaying the cumulative US debt amount.

Once the cumulative US debt amount has been repaid, the maximum income tax rate would be lowered to 40%.

Once the transformation of the federal government has been completed and the proper role of government has be re-established (i.e., protection only), the maximum income tax rate would then be lowered to the 30% tax rate.

Once our country has re-established a Self-Reliant Society, the highest marginal income tax rate would then be lowered to the 20% tax rate. When this point is reached, there would be a 10% tax on all W-2 wage income for all citizens (the 6.5% rate for Social Security, plus the 3.5% rate for Medical Care taxes). Therefore, if a taxpayer (individual or family) has taxable income above the applicable federal government poverty guideline amount, this incremental layer of income would be taxed at a maximum rate of 10%, which would be used to fund the operations of the federal government.

One of the major changes that would be accomplished with reforming the federal income tax code is to more effectively facilitate the delivery of social services (welfare) to citizens who need assistance.

These goods and services are most effectively delivered by local Not-for-Profit charitable organizations that specialize in social services.

The federal government should eliminate all federal welfare programs by 2020 (except the transformed Social Security welfare benefit) because the federal government is inferior to social service agencies in the delivery of these goods and services.

Through the use of self-directed charitable contributions to Not-for-Profit organizations, taxpayers would be allowed to satisfy a portion of their income tax obligation via their charitable contributions.

There would be three separate Charitable Contribution offset rates - a 100% tax offset for substantiated, confirmed cash contributions to four new nationally recognized Not-for-Profit charitable organizations (i.e., a national food bank, a national Habit for Humanity organization, a national medical care clearinghouse, and a national education clearinghouse – see below).

In addition, there could be other federally supported Not-for-Profit organizations, where taxpayers could get a 100% tax credit. Those Not-for-Profit organizations would need to be defined and approved by Congress (each year).

There would also be a 50% offset for substantiated, confirmed cash contributions to all other state and local Not-for-Profit charitable organizations (including religious organizations).

There would be a 10% offset for any non-cash contributions to any federal, state or local Not-for-Profit charitable organization (substantiated by Fair Market Valuations of any donated items).

Listings of the applicable federal Not-for-Profit charitable organizations would be maintained on the IRS website.

Listings of applicable state and local Not-for-Profit charitable organizations would be maintained on the applicable state's Department of Revenue website.

In order to maintain their federal tax status, all Not-for-Profit charitable organizations will have an annual federal reporting responsibility regarding the cash contributions they have received, which would be submitted to the IRS no later than January 31st. The organization's annual Form 990 would continue to be due on its normal filing date.

"Income tax preferences" (whether a deduction in the calculation of taxable income or a tax credit against the amount of tax owed) do not apply universally to all citizens, and benefit only a sub-segment of the citizenry. All income tax preferences should be eliminated, including mortgage interest expense, real estate taxes, the Earned Income Credit, the Child Tax Credit, Education credits, Residential Energy credits, etc.

As noted above, the US tax code should never again be used to "socially engineer" our country's citizens. The US income tax system should only be used to fund the operations of the federal government.

The elimination of all tax preferences, along with the changes to the taxable income ranges and income tax rates will serve to address two issues. These changes would result in more aggregate "public" funds that would be available to Not-for-Profit charities and to the federal government, so that the federal government can begin to pay off the cumulative US debt amount. The elimination of special interest groups' tax preferences, along with the introduction of a 45% income tax rate will also serve to mitigate the "noise" and negative effects on society that are attributed to the issue of "income inequality" (i.e., envy and a related sense of "entitlement").

In regards to a related tax matter, our elected officials also need to bring to closure the ongoing, never ending debate about the "death tax" (aka the estate tax). Congress needs to establish / finalize the threshold level beyond which an estate becomes taxable, along with the applicable tax rate for that taxable portion of an estate being passed from one generation to the next. The "noise" and negative effects on society that are attributed to "wealth inequality" are similar to the issues regarding "income inequality".

Our belief is that because an individual's / family's income has already been taxed once, that should be enough. However, until the cumulative US debt amount has been repaid, we believe the current threshold level and tax rate are appropriate. But having said that... a significant estate tax loophole that is currently generally available only to wealthy individuals to minimize or avoid estate/gift taxes (referred to as a Grantor Retained Annuity Trust, or GRAT) should be eliminated as soon as possible.

4 - Welfare Reform -

An individual's / family's eligibility for welfare should be assessed on an annual basis via their federal income tax return. All citizens should be accounted for each year in connection with the annual income tax return filing process.

There should be two new "check box questions" on the federal income tax return –

_____ I (we) have assessed my (our) financial situation (assets owned, less debts owed) as ofDecember 31, ____, and this net amount as of December 31st is less than the federal poverty guideline amount associated with my (our) filing status for this year's tax return

_____ I (we) request that my (our) eligibility to receive welfare assistance be reviewed with a representative of the IRS and/or Social Security Administration

Taxpayers can elect to check the first box, and if so, can then also elect to check the second box, if they so choose. Note: A change in an individual's / family's financial situation that occurs during the course of a year (due to the loss of a job, a medical situation, or any other "life event" change) can accelerate such a review, which would be initiated by the taxpayer via a phone call to the IRS and/or Social Security Administration.

The IRS agent / Social Security Administration employee will make appropriate inquiries, obtain any necessary documentation and affidavits, etc., and make a determination as to whether that individual / family is eligible for welfare, and then provide to the individual / family a reference sheet listing the local Not-for-Profit charitable organization(s) within their geographic area that best meets that individual's / family's needs.

The responsibility for overseeing the country's welfare system should reside with the Social Security Administration.

Social Security employees, working with local charitable organizations that are established to provide assistance to welfare-eligible citizens, will work with these individuals / families to help them rise above a poverty level existence.

The Federal Unemployment payroll tax should be eliminated, as there should not be any cash welfare payments.

Four new national Not-for-Profit charitable organizations should be created to collect and distribute the 100% federal income tax credits for charitable contributions. The four related federal departments (Agriculture, Housing & Urban Development, Health & Human Services, and Education).would be significantly transformed, as most of the federal government employees would move to these new national Not-for-Profit charities. These national Not-for-Profit charities would support the associated state level agencies that are tasked with the delivery of goods and services.

The four existing federal departments would continue to be overseen by the applicable cabinet level executive. But each of these federal agencies would transform itself from being an administrator / payor, and would become a clearing house regarding resources, information, and best practices that are available to assist the new national Not-for-Profit charities and the state level agencies. Each of these national charities, along with the applicable federal government departments would help address each state's funding requests, and would recommend the allocation of any additional federal government financial resources that should be sent to the states via federal block grants, which would only occur with additional oversight and approval of each year's funding by Congress.

The four existing federal departments would also oversee the IRS' approval of Not-for-Profit charitable organizations at the state and local level, which provide goods and services to our country's citizens. These four federal departments would also have oversight of the operations of the applicable agencies and, along with the IRS, would have oversight of the tax returns of the associated Not-for-Profit charitable organizations, to ensure that these public funds are being expended efficiently.

States would be allowed to maintain their own state unemployment payroll taxes if they so choose, in the event that the state wants to use their own funds to provide financial support their state's county-level Not-for-Profit charitable organizations.

Beginning in 2020, there would no longer be any federal cash welfare payments to individuals (except for the transformed, means-tested Social Security benefit).

We also recommend that there should also be no state cash welfare payments - the states should also provide only goods and services.

Individuals / families seeking welfare assistance will be given access to a listing of any open positions for employment that are available at state and local governmental units and Not-for-Profit charities.

5 - Reform / Transform Social Security over a multi-year transition period -

The federal government needs to eliminate any further reference to the Social Security Trust Funds. The only assets currently held by the Social Security Trust are "intergovernmental wealth transfer obligations" (i.e., debt). There is no cash in the Trust. Going forward, the cash flows (in and out) for Social Security should continue to simply be part of the aggregate cash flows of the federal government.

The number of active workers paying in to Social Security each year is now fewer than three workers per retiree. Life expectancy has increased significantly since Social Security was established in 1935. The current demographics of our country's population now require that fundamental changes be made to the Social Security program.

Our country needs to honor its obligation to citizens who are currently receiving Social Security pension benefits. The transformation plan needs to address the level of benefits that will be paid to citizens who are approaching retirement. All citizens (regardless of age) should receive a return of all of their payroll tax withholdings paid into Social Security, including interest at 3%. Eventually, Social Security should be transformed into a purely welfare program, available to any elderly citizen who requires such financial assistance.

The Social Security tax rate should be increased in 2020 from 6.2% to 6.5%. The wage cap limitation for Social Security taxes should be eliminated in 2020. Social Security taxes will simply be considered a portion of a citizen's total federal tax obligation each year. W-2 wages will no longer be taxed twice for both Social Security and federal income tax purposes.

Social Security disability payments should be eliminated (see Welfare Reform). If a disabled person needs financial support from someone other than their family members, that person will have welfare benefits available to them, if they choose to elect to receive such benefits, by making the appropriate notation on their annual federal income tax return. If approved for welfare, they will have access to the Not-for-Profit charitable organizations that specialize in mitigating their disability.

The financial administration of the Social Security system should be significantly simplified. Eventually (once Social Security has been transformed into a means-tested welfare benefit) the annual benefit should be capped at an amount equal to the applicable federal poverty guideline amount. If an individual needs to receive this welfare benefit, such a benefit would begin at the person's full retirement age (without exception). The current program feature that allows a person to receive reduced Social Security benefits early, or to receive an enhanced benefit later by electing to defer the start of benefits, should be eliminated. Citizens should make their personal financial plans based on the knowledge that they will be entitled to receive a known welfare benefit (if necessary), capped at the federal poverty guideline amount, beginning at their full retirement age. As is the case currently, people can continue to retire early, or delay their retirement, according to their own personal choice.

The following comments represent a recommended transformation plan over a multi-year transition period -

Beginning in 2020, the 6.5% payroll tax withholdings for Social Security would be used to satisfy a portion of an individual's / family's federal income tax obligations.

Beginning in 2020, all social security benefits received should be included in the calculation of taxable income.

Beginning in 2020, the full retirement age (which would apply to all citizens) would increase to age 68, and would be subsequently "indexed" based on subsequent changes in life expectancy.

Our country needs to continue to honor its commitments to all retirees who are receiving Social Security benefits in 2020. These retirees' Social Security benefit would be grandfathered under the old rules, including their entitlement to future Cost of Living increases based on an annual inflation rate. This would include any individual who is less than 68 years old, who elected to start receiving reduced benefits early before their full retirement age.

Similarly, any person who is 64 as of January 1, 2016 (68 as of January 1, 2020) would also be grandfathered under the old rules. However, if their Social Security benefit exceeds the federal poverty guideline amount, there would be no "COLA" increase to their Social Security benefit until the federal poverty guideline amount begins to exceed their Social Security benefit.

Individuals who are between age 58 and 63 as of January 1, 2016 would be covered by new transition rules. These rules would guarantee a minimum percentage of the higher benefit level that would otherwise have been available to them under the old rules. In all cases, each person would be entitled to receive (regardless of any means testing) a Social Security benefit amount at least equal to the federal poverty guideline amount. Someone age 63 would be guaranteed 90% of the benefit available under the old plan. Someone age 62 would be guaranteed 80%, someone age 61 would be guaranteed 70%, and those individuals between age 58 to age 60 would be guaranteed 60% of the benefit available under the old plan (in all cases, provided that the guaranteed amount so determined is at least equal to the federal poverty guideline amount).

Individuals who are younger than age 58 as of January 1, 2016 would need to make their financial plans under the new rules that would be in effect starting in 2020. Generally, these citizens would only be able to receive a Social

Security welfare benefit (starting at age 68) if their annual "means test" (as indicated on their federal income tax return) shows that they are eligible for welfare. However, under the Social Security transition rules, all citizens who are younger than age 58 as of January 1, 2016 would be entitled to receive a refund (starting at age 68) of all of their social security payroll tax withholdings that they contributed into Social Security via their payroll tax withholdings through the year ending December 31, 2019. [As noted above, starting in 2020, Social Security payroll tax withholdings will be used to satisfy a portion of a taxpayer's total federal income tax liability each year.] Interest compounded using a 3% interest rate would be added to these Social Security payroll tax withholdings through 2019, and this total would be refunded to the individual, starting at age 68.

When an individual reaches age 68, they would begin to receive a Social Security benefit equal to the federal poverty guideline amount. Similar to the existing rules for social security, benefits would cease at death, even if the individual had not yet received the full amount that they had paid into Social Security. However, once they have received the total amount that they paid into Social Security via their payroll tax withholdings through the year 2019 (including accrued interest), their benefits would cease (unless they are eligible for welfare at that point in time).

Once the country's social security program has been transformed, the original intent of providing a "financial security" benefit to elderly retirees who qualify for welfare will have been re-established. If an elderly retiree indicates on their annual federal income tax return that they qualify for welfare (and if upon review, this eligibility is confirmed), they would be entitled to receive a Social Security welfare benefit equal to the federal poverty guideline amount.

6 - Reform the US Healthcare system -

Similar to Social Security, the federal government needs to eliminate any further reference to the Medicare Trust Funds, as the only assets currently held by the Medicare Trust are "intergenerational wealth transfer obligations" (i.e., debt).

Starting in 2020, our country should implement a private sector versus public sector healthcare system that would be applicable to all US citizens, whether they are below age 68 or are Medicare-age-eligible. The primary healthcare delivery system will continue to be the existing commercial, private sector health insurance system, which is a regulated industry at the state level. The other option would be a transformed Medicaid option that would provide

68

coverage under a nationalized, public (welfare) healthcare delivery system, administered at the state level, with bronze level coverages.

Starting in 2020, all Medical Care payroll tax withholdings collected by the federal government will be immediately remitted back to the applicable state. Each state would also be eligible to receive a "per welfare recipient" portion of the national Not-for-Profit charity that has been established to receive voluntary charitable contributions from our country's citizens.

Starting in 2020, the Medical Care payroll tax rate would be increased from 1.45% to 3.5%. All federal payroll tax withholdings and employer payroll taxes for Medical Care that are collected by the federal government would be immediately remitted directly back to the applicable state.

Starting in 2020, state governments, along with the applicable associated social service agencies within the state, would become responsible for overseeing the delivery of healthcare to their state's citizens. As noted above, additional financial support, over and above that state's payroll tax withholdings and that state's portion of the national charity's receipts, would be provided to the state by the federal government, if needed.

Until all states are self-sufficient in delivering the minimum level of care to its citizens, appropriate federal support (as approved by the US House of Representatives and US Senate) will be provided to each state each year in the form of a federal block grant. This block grant will be determined based on each state's demographics and the number of its citizens living below the federal poverty level.

The Department of Health and Human Services will determine the minimum healthcare entitlements of all US citizens (subject to approval by the US House of Representatives and the US Senate). This entitlement would be available under the public (welfare) bronze level healthcare option, available from the state, for those individuals/families who want to elect that level of coverage. The premium cost for this type of bronze level coverage will be established by the Department of Health and Human Services, subject to approval by the US House of Representatives and the US Senate, and this premium cost for the bronze level public health insurance coverage would be incorporated into the federal poverty guideline amount for individuals / various family sizes.

Similarly, the aggregate, total federal poverty guideline amount(s) for individuals / various family sizes (which includes the cost of food, housing, medical care, etc.) would continue to be established by the Department of

Health and Human Services, subject to annual review and approval by the US House of Representatives and US Senate.

State health insurance exchanges would continue to be the market place for employer-provided health plans, and for private health insurance policies for those individuals / families who are not covered by an employer-provided plan. The state's insurance regulators would continue to oversee the health insurance marketplace within that state, similar to practices in place today.

Individuals / families would be free to obtain their insurance coverage from their employer (if so offered, and if they so choose) or they can elect to own their own insurance policy, similar to any other type of insurance they acquire. Citizens should be allowed to acquire their own private health insurance policy from any insurance company in the country, including from an insurance company in another state, if that is the choice they would like to make.

Health insurance companies would continue to be free to offer Silver and Gold coverage plans to employers and individuals under the states' health insurance exchanges, similar to what they do today.

Individuals / families would continue to have the right to choose to pay higher premiums, and acquire a silver or gold level health insurance policy that has enhanced health insurance benefits / additional protections if that is what they choose to acquire.

In order to level the playing field between employed persons and self-employed persons, the value of employer-provided health insurance (including the value of any employer funded health insurance cost paid to an employee's union) would be included as wages on an employee's W-2.

Similarly, the value of governmental-agency-provided health insurance would be included as wages on the W-2s issued to public sector employees.

The US Supreme Court has ruled that the obligation to pay the cost of health insurance is a tax. Accordingly, in the event that an individual / family is not covered by health insurance during the year, the bronze level health insurance premium amount (as established by the Department of Health and Human Services and approved by Congress) would be collected via that individual's / family's federal income tax return, and any such tax amount collected by the federal government would be immediately remitted directly back to the applicable state.

The age for Medicare eligibility would increase from the current age 65 to age 68 by the year 2020, so that Medicare would match the full retirement age established for Social Security. The Department of Health and Human Services (subject to approval by the US House of Representatives and US Senate) would determine the minimum healthcare entitlements of citizens eligible for Medicare. This would become the bronze level of coverage available under Medicare.

The Department of Health and Human Services (subject to approval by the US House of Representatives and US Senate) would also determine the Medicare premium cost for this bronze level of coverage, which citizens would pay to their state's healthcare program, for their particular Medicare insurance plan.

Medicare-eligible citizens would continue to be able to purchase Medicare supplemental insurance coverage policies, if that is what they choose to do. Accordingly, beginning in 2020, Medicare would be transformed into a premium-support program. From a risk management and cost perspective, healthcare costs for retirees over age 68 would initially in 2020 be borne 75% by Medicare (the other costs being covered by Medicare supplemental insurance coverage policies and / or personally). This premium support level would then be reduced by 5% each year for the next 3 years until eventually in 2023, 60% of the healthcare costs for citizens over age 68 would be borne by the public (taxpayers) and 40% would be a Personal Responsibility.

In order to address a major concern regarding our country's annual healthcare cost, bronze level coverage would primarily be established to cover a routine annual health exam, and would provide coverage for a major life threatening catastrophic event. As noted above, these coverages would be established by the Department of Health and Human Services, subject to approval by the US House of Representatives and the US Senate. Under the nationalized bronze level coverages, there would be a requirement that only generic prescription drugs be covered, and there would be significant state government oversight / approval of the services to be provided under the bronze level policy. In addition, there would be a major emphasis on preventive care under a bronze level policy. Many of these bronze level services would be provided by Not-for-Profit charitable organizations (which will be financially supported by changes to federal income tax policies regarding charitable contributions) which would fulfill various specific niche needs.

A key cultural change that needs to be implemented in connection with bronze level coverage is in regards to tort reform and legal liability protections. To ensure that state and local healthcare providers will be able to deliver these bronze level healthcare services at the lowest possible cost, there should be significant legal liability protections offered to those doctors and service providers and the affiliated Not-for-Profit charitable organizations. Individuals / families who opt for bronze level coverage under the nationalized, public (welfare) healthcare option would need to be made aware that they are receiving these medical care services at "below market" cost, and therefore their ability to initiate damages claims against the government will be severely limited. It is recognized that unfavorable medical outcomes will inevitably occur - - any such matters / instances would initially be addressed at the state level, and the oversight of the states' processes to deal with these matters would be overseen at the federal level by a unit within the Department of Health and Human Services.

Note: The 2020 Initiative was originally written during 2015. Because of Congress' delay in addressing the federal government's growing debt problem, the suggested dates in this document will probably need to be pushed back by two years, to continue to give our country's citizens enough time to adjust their financial plans, so that they can take into consideration these comprehensive, inter-related changes.

Fair versus Unfortunate

Our Editorial Board recently had an interesting conversation about the concepts of "Fair" and "Unfortunate".

Much of the political debate within our country over the past several years has revolved around the issue of what is fair. But before we address that question, we should first re-emphasize that our Editorial Board believes the primary focus of the federal government should be directed "outward" - - towards our country's relationships with other countries in the world. The federal government's primary role is one of protection – protecting the country as a whole (not special interest groups). We feel that many of our country's political problems have arisen since the 1960s because the federal government's focus has become redirected towards "internal" issues. "Progressives" feel that the federal government should be free to initiate and grow any program that is needed to "solve" any problem that the government decides needs to be fixed, including whatever issue the government deems to be unfair.

Interestingly, the issue of fairness was evoked eleven times during the Democratic debate on October 13, 2015, and fiscal responsibility was mentioned only once (by Lincoln Chafee). The country's growing debt problem was not mentioned once during the Democratic debate, so there was never any chance to discuss whether this issue is fair to future generations. (But we digress)...

One of the key problems with the issue of fairness is that it entails a "values judgment". One person's definition of what is fair might not be the same as the next person's. So you spend a lot of time and energy trying to convince someone else that your definition of fairness is correct. In order to resolve a situation that someone deems to be unfair, you need to "trade resources" between individuals - - you need to take something away from someone, to give it to another, to make things fair. If you take this line of thinking to its logical conclusion, the only answer to the question of fairness (in regards to economic issues) is that Communism is the only solution that is truly fair. Unfortunately (fortunately?) history has provided definitive proof that Communism is not the solution to the issue of fairness. So if the solution is not Communism, is the answer to the fairness question Senator Bernie Sanders' proposals for "Democratic Socialism"? We think not.

We believe that it is impossible for a government to engineer fairness. We are also sure that one of the Pearls of Wisdom that your mother passed on to you at a very young age is that "Life is not fair". The progressive agenda is devoted towards trying to prove that your mother is wrong.

There is a fundamental difference between "fair" and "unfortunate". Is it unfair, say, that your passion in life is to play basketball in the NBA, but you're only 5'8" tall (and you don't have the skills)? Unfortunately, this is unfortunate. Is it unfair that you would like to live in a 15,000 square foot house with a full-size indoor basketball court, but you don't have the financial means? Is it unfair that there are people who do have the physical skills to play in the NBA and/or live in a 15,000 square foot house with a full-size indoor basketball court? We believe that most people would answer this last question "No, this is not unfair".

We recognize that the above illustration is a bit extreme. So let's bring the issue down to the context of "life's bare necessities" (food, shelter, education, healthcare). Is it unfair that because of your level of education, your skills, or some other aspect of your personal life, that it is difficult for you to earn a "median" annual income that is above the federal poverty guideline amount? We don't believe that this is unfair, but we agree that this is probably unfortunate.

So what is the federal government's role in regards to "fair" versus "unfortunate"?

In regards to "fair" - - we believe that the federal government has a responsibility to support the concept of "Opportunity for All, Favoritism to None". We believe the government has a role to play to ensure that all Americans live in a society that has a level playing field - an equal opportunity (not necessarily an equal end result). This was one of the positive outcomes that came out of the country's civil rights movement during the 1960s. America has eliminated many of the laws that were being used to maintain a tilted playing field. The flip side of equal opportunity is that the government should not foster any favoritism towards any "subset" of the population. This would include homeowners versus renters, public servants versus people who work in the private sector, members of any particular religion or any particular racial group, people with a particular disability (more on this later), Wall Street firms, banks that are too big to fail, oil companies, solar energy companies, wind energy companies, labor unions, companies that export products to other countries, etc.

In regards to "unfortunate" - - we believe that the federal government does not have a direct role to play, because it is not possible for the government to solve any particular individual's personal issue. However, as we mention in The

2020 Initiative, we do believe that the federal government does have a role to play via its income tax policies, to ensure that appropriate funds are available to Not-for-Profit charitable organizations, so that those organizations can fulfill their mission to provide social services to any and all citizens who need assistance. This is the role of civil society (families, supported by friends and neighbors, religious organizations, and Not-for-Profit charitable organizations). The federal government should eliminate all of its programs that attempt to solve every unfortunate situation. The federal government's poverty programs have been an abject failure. Local food banks, Habitat for Humanity organizations, educational Not-for-Profit organizations, medical Not-for-Profit organizations, and other social service agencies that provide specific, targeted solutions are a much better option, compared to any program run by the federal government.

A Right versus A Personal Responsibility

Bernie Sanders and Hillary Clinton both made an interesting assertion during the Democratic presidential candidate debate on October 13, 2015 - - Healthcare is a right, and it should be made available to all citizens by the federal government.

If you are reading this Conversation Piece, you probably have access to our Foundation's very first Conversation Piece entitled *Why Mitt Romney's Comments About the 47% Were Not Correct.* While Mr. Romney made some erroneous assertions during his fund raising event in May 2012, he also made some very appropriate comments, too, one of which was…. *there are [citizens] who are with him [Obama], who are dependent upon government, who believe… the government has a responsibility to care for them, who believe that they are entitled to healthcare, to food, to housing, to you-name-it. That's an entitlement. The government should give it to them.*

Unfortunately, Bernie Sanders and Hillary Clinton (and others within the liberal / progressive movement) continue to pursue this agenda. The issue of defining what constitutes a "right" (to which everyone is entitled) is one of the most fundamental distinctions between the two political parties, and is one of the defining issues that needs to be resolved during the upcoming 2016 presidential election.

But why stop with just healthcare?
If food is a right, is hamburger a right? (Is a steak a right? Is a lobster dinner a right?)

If housing is a right, is a 700 square foot apartment a right? (Is a 2,000 square foot condo a right? Is a 15,000 square foot house on 5 acres of land a right?)

Unfortunately, much of the political debate within our country over the past several years has been centered on the issue of what is "fair". As we note in our Conversation Piece entitled *"Fair versus Unfortunate"*, the problem with the government trying to achieve "fairness" is that it entails a debate about a "values judgment". One person's definition of what is fair is oftentimes not the same as the next person's.

Our Editorial Board believes that our country is having the wrong conversation. Instead of debating "fairness", we should be having a conversation about the distinction between a right versus a Personal Responsibility. (And because we are The Foundation to Promote Personal Responsibility, you can probably guess what our answer to this question would be).

Unfortunately, the liberal / progressive movement knows no boundaries. The progressives achieved their first major success in 1935, by granting a right (an "entitlement") to a stream of money from the government during retirement. And unfortunately, Social Security is fundamentally flawed in that it pays the wrong amount of money to the wrong people. The real question is, Why did FDR and the federal government feel compelled to remove the responsibility for providing for your own retirement from the list of things for which you have your own Personal Responsibility?

We agree that our country is prosperous enough, so that no citizen should ever face death because of the lack of the bare necessities (food, housing, medical care, etc). However, each of these things represents a Personal Responsibility. It is unfortunate that some people will inevitably struggle to stay out of poverty. In those situations, civil society (families, supported by friends, neighbors, religious groups and Not-for-Profit charitable organizations) (not the federal government) should ensure that "social security" is available to any citizen who needs assistance.

Progressives fail to recognize (or fail to acknowledge) that nothing in life is "free". And unfortunately, the citizens who will end up paying for the liberal / progressive agenda are our children and grandchildren. This is especially true for any government program that is not paid for currently, but instead is financed by borrowing from future generations.

There is a fundamental distinction between a right and a Personal Responsibility. This is the conversation that Mitt Romney was trying to initiate back in 2012, and it is the conversation that we need to continue to have during 2016, because unfortunately (yes, we're repeating ourselves here) the liberal / progressive movement knows no boundaries.

Thomas Paine and Common Sense

As we have noted elsewhere on our website, one of the most important decisions that will be made during the upcoming 2016 presidential election is whether our country will continue to move towards socialism and an ever-expanding federal government, or whether We-the-People will exercise Common Sense and begin to return to the principles that were put forward by our country's Founders.

In 1776, Thomas Paine published a pamphlet entitled *Common Sense*. The following is an extract from some of the opening paragraphs -

Some writers have so confounded society with government, as to leave little or no distinction between them; whereas they are not only different, but have different origins. Society is produced by our want, and government by our wickedness; the former promotes our happiness POSITIVELY by uniting our affections, the latter NEGATIVELY by restraining our vices.

Society in every state is a blessing, but Government, even in its best state, is but a necessary evil; in its worst state an intolerable one.... Wherefore, security being the true design and end of government, it unanswerably follows that whatever form thereof appears most likely to ensure it to us, with the least expense and greatest benefit, is preferable to all others....

In the following pages I offer nothing more than simple facts, plain arguments, and common sense....

(Setting aside his use of the King's English) Mr. Paine was simply saying that there is a fundamental difference between civil society (the individual and families and "communities") and society's need to establish a government to provide security and protect the country's citizens (with the least amount of expense).

This is one of those self-evident truths that hasn't changed over the years. We just need to remember that there is a fundamental difference between civil society and government (and then go exercise some Common Sense).

The US Constitution   Article 1   Section 8

The Congress shall have Power To lay and collect Taxes, Duties, Imposts and Excises, to pay the Debts and provide for the common Defence and general Welfare of the United States; but all Duties, Imposts and Excises shall be uniform throughout the United States;

To borrow Money on the credit of the United States;

To regulate Commerce with foreign Nations, and among the several States, and with the Indian Tribes;

To establish an uniform Rule of Naturalization, and uniform Laws on the subject of Bankruptcies throughout the United States;

To coin Money, regulate the Value thereof, and of foreign Coin, and fix the Standard of Weights and Measures;

To provide for the Punishment of counterfeiting the Securities and current Coin of the United States;

To establish Post Offices and post Roads;

To promote the Progress of Science and useful Arts, by securing for limited Times to Authors and Inventors the exclusive Right to their respective Writings and Discoveries;

To constitute Tribunals inferior to the supreme Court;

To define and punish Piracies and Felonies committed on the high Seas, and Offences against the Law of Nations;

To declare War, grant Letters of Marque and Reprisal, and make Rules concerning Captures on Land and Water;

To raise and support Armies, but no Appropriation of Money to that Use shall be for a longer Term than two Years;

To provide and maintain a Navy;

To make Rules for the Government and Regulation of the land and naval Forces;

To provide for calling forth the Militia to execute the Laws of the Union, suppress Insurrections and repel Invasions;

To provide for organizing, arming, and disciplining, the Militia, and for governing such Part of them as may be employed in the Service of the United States, reserving to the States respectively, the Appointment of the Officers, and the Authority of training the Militia according to the discipline prescribed by Congress;

To exercise exclusive Legislation in all Cases whatsoever, over such District (not exceeding ten Miles square) as may, by Cession of particular States, and the Acceptance of Congress, become the Seat of the Government of the United States, and to exercise like Authority over all Places purchased by the Consent of the Legislature of the State in which the Same shall be, for the Erection of Forts, Magazines, Arsenals, dock-Yards, and other needful Buildings; and

To make all Laws which shall be necessary and proper for carrying into Execution the foregoing Powers, and all other Powers vested by this Constitution in the Government of the United States, or in any Department or Officer thereof.

Pearls of Wisdom

On Personal Responsibility -

Nothing in this world can take the place of persistence. Talent will not - nothing is more common than unsuccessful men with talent. Genius will not - unrewarded genius is almost a proverb. Education will not - the world is full of educated derelicts. Persistence and determination alone are omnipotent. – Calvin Coolidge

Always bear in mind that your own resolution to succeed is more important than any other one thing. - Abraham Lincoln

When you do nothing, you feel overwhelmed and powerless. But when you get involved, you feel the sense of hope and accomplishment that comes from knowing you are working to make things better. - Albert Einstein

Everyone can rise above their circumstances and achieve success if they are dedicated to and passionate about what they do. - Nelson Mandela

As my sufferings mounted I soon realized that there were two ways in which I could respond to my situation -- either to react with bitterness or seek to transform the suffering into a creative force. I decided to follow the latter course. - Martin Luther King Jr.

You were not born a winner, and you were not born a loser. You are what you make yourself be. – Lou Holtz

It's hard to beat a person who never gives up. - Babe Ruth

Achievement is largely the product of steadily raising one's levels of aspiration and expectation. - Jack Nicklaus

People who are unable to motivate themselves must be content with mediocrity, no matter how impressive their other talents. - Andrew Carnegie

How wonderful it is that nobody need wait a single moment before starting to improve the world. - Anne Frank

Hope never abandons you, you abandon it. – George Weinberg

I always wondered why somebody doesn't do something about that. Then I realized I was somebody. – Lily Tomlin

Don't expect to improve the weak by tearing down the strong. – Calvin Coolidge

You cannot strengthen the weak by weakening the strong. You cannot help the wage earner by pulling down the wage payer. You cannot help the poor by destroying the rich. You cannot help men permanently by doing for them what they could and should do for themselves. – The Rev. William John Henry Boetcker

Even if you're on the right track, you'll get run over if you just sit there. - Will Rogers

On Government and Debt -

The best government is that which governs least. – Thomas Jefferson

We are a nation that has a government – not the other way around. And this makes us special among the nations of the Earth. Our government has no power except that granted it by the people. It is time to check and reverse the growth of government which shows sign of having grown beyond the consent of the governed. – Ronald Reagan

80

Good intentions will always be pleaded for every assumption of authority. It is hardly too strong to say that the Constitution was made to guard the people against the dangers of good intentions. There are men in all ages who meant to govern well, but they mean to govern. They promise to be good masters, but they mean to be masters. – Noah Webster

There is no nation on earth powerful enough to accomplish our overthrow. Or destruction, should it come at all, will be from the inattention of the people to the concerns of their government. – Daniel Webster

There is no "slippery slope" toward loss of liberties, only a long staircase where each step downward must first be tolerated by the American people and their leaders. – Alan K. Simpson

The Constitution is NOT an instrument for the government to restrain the people; it is an instrument for the people to restrain the government, lest it come to dominate our lives and interests. – Patrick Henry

Government's first duty is to protect the people, not to run their lives. – Ronald Reagan

We have a system that increasingly taxes work and subsidizes non-work. – Milton Friedman

There is far more danger in public than private monopoly, for when government goes into business it can always shift its losses to the taxpayer. Government never makes ends meet, and that is the first requisite of business. – Thomas Edison

There are two ways to conquer and enslave a country. One is by the sword. The other is by debt. – Jon Adams

I predict future happiness for Americans if they can prevent the government from wasting the labors of the people under the pretense of taking care of them. –Thomas Jefferson

I, however, place economy among the first and most important of republican virtues, and public debt as the greatest of dangers to be feared. — Thomas Jefferson

Think what you do when you run in debt - you give to another the power over your liberty. - Benjamin Franklin

Democracy extends the sphere of individual freedom, socialism restricts it. Democracy attaches all possible value to each man; socialism makes each man a mere agent, a mere number. Democracy and socialism have nothing in common but one word: equality. But notice the difference: while democracy seeks equality in liberty, socialism seeks equality in restraint and servitude. - Alexis de Tocqueville

The health of a democratic society may be measured by the quality of functions performed by private citizens. - Alexis de Tocqueville

America will never by destroyed from the outside. If we falter and lose our freedoms, it will be because we destroyed ourselves. - Abraham Lincoln

I wish it were possible to obtain a single amendment to our constitution; I would be willing to depend on that alone for the reduction of the administration of our government to the genuine principles of its constitution; I mean an additional article taking from the federal government the power of borrowing. - Thomas Jefferson

Avoid likewise the accumulation of debt, not only by shunning occasions of expense, but [also] by vigorous exertions in time of peace to discharge the debts which unavoidable wars have occasioned, not ungenerously throwing upon posterity the burden which we ourselves ought to bear. - George Washington

Let every man, every corporation and especially let every village, town and city, every county and State, get out of debt and keep out of debt. It is the debtor that is ruined by hard times. - Rutherford B. Hayes

We don't have a [multi-] trillion-dollar debt because we haven't taxed enough. We have a [multi-] trillion-dollar debt because we spend too much. - Ronald Reagan

We contend that for a nation to try to tax itself into prosperity is like a man standing in a bucket and trying to lift himself up by the handle. - Winston Churchill

The problem with Socialism is that you eventually run out of other people's money. - Margaret Thatcher

Other Quotes –

82

And so, my fellow Americans, ask not what your country can do for you, ask what you can do for your country. - John F. Kennedy

Freedom is never more than one generation away from extinction. We didn't pass it to our children in the bloodstream. It must be fought for, protected, and handed on for them to do the same. - Ronald Reagan

The people of these United States are the rightful masters of both Congresses and courts, not to overthrow the Constitution, but to overthrow the men who pervert the Constitution. - Abraham Lincoln

The States are separate and independent sovereigns. Sometimes they need to act like it. – Chief Justice John Roberts

Never do anything against conscience even if the state demands it. – Albert Einstein

The ultimate test of man's conscience may be his willingness to sacrifice something today for future generations whose words of thanks will not be heard. - Gaylord Nelson

Right is right, even if everyone is against it, and wrong is wrong, even if everyone is for it. – William Penn
[Our message to the 435 members of the House of Representatives and 100 US Senators - - Stealing from our children and grandkids is morally wrong.]

Be brave enough to start a conversation that matters. - Margaret Wheatley

You need only reflect that one of the best ways to get yourself a reputation as a dangerous citizen these days is to go about repeating the very phrases which our founding fathers used in the great struggle for independence. – Charles Austin Beard

Education is the most powerful weapon which you can use to change the world. - Nelson Mandela

Those who do not learn from history are doomed to repeat it. – George Santayana

Live as if you were going to die tomorrow. Learn as if you were going to live forever. – Mahatma Gandhi

In matters of style, swim with the current; in matters of principle, stand like a rock. - Thomas Jefferson

I have never understood why it is "greed" to want to keep the money you've earned, but not greed to want to take somebody else's money. - Thomas Sowell

And then some more -

The nine most terrifying words in the English language are "I'm from the government, and I'm here to help."
- Ronald Reagan

If you put our federal government in charge of the Sahara Desert, in five years there would be a shortage of sand. - Milton Friedman

Blessed are the young, for they shall inherit the national debt. - Herbert Hoover

Government is like a baby. An alimentary canal with a big appetite at one end and no sense of responsibility at the other. - Ronald Reagan

There are 249 millionaires in Congress. Remember a couple of years ago when this new Congress told us they had the solution to the recession? Apparently, they didn't share it with the rest of us. - Jay Leno

Yesterday Obama presented a $4 trillion budget that he says would help the middle class. Then the middle class said, "You know what? How about you just give us the $4 trillion? We'll figure out what to do with it." - Jimmy Fallon

We're learning more about the dead Venezuelan dictator Hugo Chavez. It seems he amassed about $2 billion in personal fortune while president, and he was a socialist. Just imagine how rich he could have been if he didn't believe in redistribution of wealth. - Jay Leno

If Patrick Henry thought that taxation without representation was bad, he should see how bad it is with representation. - Farmer's Almanac

I wouldn't mind paying taxes - if I knew they were going to a friendly country. - Dick Gregory

84

Income tax returns are the most imaginative fiction being written today.
- Herman Wouk

The income tax has made more liars out of the American people than golf has.
- Will Rogers

The taxpayer - that's someone who works for the federal government but
doesn't have to take the civil service examination. - Ronald Reagan

A government that robs Peter to pay Paul can always depend on the support
of Paul. - George Bernard Shaw

Any man who thinks he can be happy and prosperous by letting the
Government take care of him,
better take a closer look at the American Indian. - Henry Ford

We have to pass the Healthcare bill so that you can find out what is in it. -
Nancy Pelosi

THE PARTY OF PERSONAL FREEDOM - *Our Platform*

PREAMBLE

The members of THE PARTY OF PERSONAL FREEDOM, along with the
members of The Foundation to Promote Personal Responsibility
(www.F2PPR.org), seek a world in which all individuals are sovereign over
their own lives and no one is forced to sacrifice his or her values for the benefit
of others.

We believe that respect for individual rights is the essential precondition for a
free and prosperous world, that force and fraud must be banished from
human relationships, and that only through freedom can peace and prosperity
be realized.

Consequently, we defend each person's right to engage in any activity that is
peaceful and honest, and welcome the diversity that freedom brings. The
world we seek to build is one where individuals are free to follow their own
dreams in their own ways, without interference from government or any
authoritarian power, and accordingly accept Personal Responsibility for the
consequences of the choices that they make.

In the following pages we have set forth our basic principles and enumerated various policy stands derived from those principles.

These specific policies are not our goal, however. Our goal is nothing more nor less than a world set free in our lifetime, and it is to this end that we take these stands.

STATEMENT OF PRINCIPLES

We, the members of THE PARTY OF PERSONAL FREEDOM, challenge the cult of the omnipotent state and defend the rights of the individual. We reject the Liberal / Progressive agenda and seek to reduce the size and scope of the federal government. We want a federal government so small that you can barely see it. We seek to re-establish the proper role of the federal government as laid out in Article 1, Section 8 of the US Constitution.

We hold that all individuals have the right to exercise sole dominion over their own lives, and have the right to live in whatever manner they choose, so long as they do not forcibly interfere with the equal right of others to live in whatever manner they choose.

Governments throughout history have regularly operated on the opposite principle, that the State has the right to dispose of the lives of individuals and the fruits of their labor. Even within the United States, all political parties other than our own grant to government the right to regulate the lives of individuals and seize the fruits of their labor without their consent.

We, on the contrary, deny the right of any government to do these things, and hold that where governments exist, they must not violate the rights of any individual: namely, (1) the right to life -- accordingly we support the prohibition of the initiation of physical force against others; (2) the right to liberty of speech and action -- accordingly we oppose all attempts by government to abridge the freedom of speech and press, as well as government censorship in any form; and (3) the right to property -- accordingly we oppose any government interference with the right to private property, and support the prohibition of robbery, trespass, fraud, and misrepresentation.

Since governments, when instituted, must not violate individual rights, we oppose all interference by government in the areas of voluntary and contractual relations among individuals. People should not be forced to sacrifice their lives and property for the benefit of others. They should be left free by government to deal with one another as free traders; and the resultant economic system, the only one compatible with the protection of individual rights, is the free market.

1.0 Personal Liberty and Responsibility

Individuals should be free to make choices for themselves and to accept Personal Responsibility for the consequences of the choices they make. Our support of an individual's right to make choices in life does not mean that we necessarily approve or disapprove of those choices. No individual, group, or government may initiate force against any other individual, group, or government.

1.1 Self-Ownership

Individuals own their bodies and have rights over them that other individuals, groups, and governments may not violate. Individuals have the freedom and responsibility to decide what they knowingly and voluntarily consume, and what risks they accept to their own health, finances, safety, or life.

1.2 Expression and Communication

We support full freedom of expression and oppose government censorship, regulation or control of communications media and technology. We favor the freedom to engage in or abstain from any religious activities that do not violate the rights of others. We oppose government actions which either aid or attack any religion.

1.3 Privacy

Members of THE PARTY OF PERSONAL FREEDOM advocate individual privacy and government transparency. We are committed to ending the government's intrusion on personal privacy. We support the rights recognized by the Fourth Amendment to be secure in our persons, homes, property, and communications. Protection from unreasonable search and seizure should include records held by third parties, such as email, medical, and library records.

1.4 Personal Relationships

Sexual orientation, preference, gender, or gender identity should have no impact on the government's treatment of individuals, such as in current marriage, child custody, adoption, immigration or military service laws. Government does not have the authority to define, license or restrict personal relationships. Consenting adults should be free to choose their own sexual practices and personal relationships.

1.5 Abortion

Recognizing that abortion is a sensitive issue and that people can hold good-faith views on all sides, we believe that government should be kept out of this matter entirely, leaving the question to each person for their conscientious consideration. No government funds should ever be expended to provide for abortions.

1.6 Crime and Justice

Government exists to protect the rights of every individual including life, liberty and property. Criminal laws should be limited to violation of the rights of others through force or fraud, or deliberate actions that place others involuntarily at significant risk of harm. We favor the repeal of all laws creating "crimes" without victims, such as the use of drugs for medicinal or recreational purposes, since only actions that infringe on the rights of others can properly be termed crimes. Individuals retain the right to voluntarily assume risk of harm to themselves. We support restitution to the victim to the fullest degree possible at the expense of the criminal or the negligent wrongdoer. We oppose reduction of constitutional safeguards of the rights of the criminally accused. The rights of due process, a speedy trial, legal counsel, trial by jury, and the legal presumption of innocence until proven guilty, must not be denied. We assert the common-law right of juries to judge not only the facts but also the justice of the law.

1.7 Self-Defense

The only legitimate use of force is in defense of individual rights — life, liberty, and justly acquired property — against aggression. This right inheres in the individual, who may agree to be aided by any other individual or group. We affirm the individual right recognized by the Second Amendment to keep and bear arms, and oppose the prosecution of individuals for exercising their rights of self-defense. Private property owners should be free to establish their own conditions regarding the presence of personal defense weapons on their own property. We oppose all laws at any level of government restricting, registering, or monitoring the ownership, manufacture, or transfer of firearms or ammunition.

2.0 Economic Liberty

Members of THE PARTY OF PERSONAL FREEDOM want all members of society to have abundant opportunities to achieve economic success. A free and competitive market allocates resources in the most efficient manner. Each person has the right to offer goods and services to others on the free market. The only proper role of government in the economic realm is to protect property rights, adjudicate disputes, and provide a legal framework in which voluntary trade is protected. All efforts by government to redistribute wealth, or to control or manage trade, are improper in a free society.

2.1 Property and Contract

Because respect for property rights is fundamental to maintaining a free and prosperous society, it follows that the freedom to contract to obtain, retain, profit from, manage, or dispose of one's property must also be upheld. Our party's members would free property owners from government restrictions on their rights to control and enjoy their property, as long as their choices do not harm or infringe on the rights of others. Governmental controls on prices of goods and services (including wages, rents, and interest) are abridgements of such fundamental rights. For voluntary dealings among private entities, parties should be free to choose with whom they trade and set whatever trade terms are mutually agreeable.

2.2 Environment

Members of THE PARTY OF PERSONAL FREEDOM support a clean and healthy environment and sensible use of our natural resources. Private landowners and conservation groups have a vested interest in maintaining natural resources. Pollution and misuse of resources cause damage to our ecosystem. Governments, unlike private businesses, are unaccountable for such damage done to our environment and have a terrible track record when it comes to environmental protection. Protecting the environment requires a clear definition and enforcement of individual rights in resources like land, water, air, and wildlife, and needs to be combined with appropriate governmental oversight of maximum pollution levels that should not be exceeded. States should be free to set lower limits, if that is what a particular state would like to do. The day to day administration of environmental regulations should be performed by the states and not the federal government.

Free markets and property rights stimulate the technological innovations and behavioral changes required to protect our environment and ecosystems. We realize that our planet's climate is constantly changing, but environmental advocates and social pressure are the most effective means of changing public behavior.

2.3 Energy and Resources

While energy is needed to fuel a modern society, government should not be subsidizing any particular form of energy. We oppose all government control of energy pricing, allocation, and production.

2.4 Government Finance and Spending

All persons are entitled to keep the fruits of their labor. We call for a complete re-writing of federal income tax policies for personal income taxes and the abolishment of all federal programs and services not required under the US Constitution. Government should not incur debt, which burdens future generations, as they have not provided their consent. We support the passage of a "Balanced Budget Amendment" to the US Constitution, provided that the budget is balanced exclusively by cutting expenditures, and not by raising taxes.

2.5 Money and Financial Markets

We favor free-market banking, with unrestricted competition among banks and depository institutions of all types. Markets are not actually free unless fraud is vigorously combated and neither profits nor losses are socialized. Individuals engaged in voluntary exchange should be free to use as money any mutually agreeable commodity or item. We support a halt to inflationary monetary policies and unconstitutional legal tender laws.

2.6 Marketplace Freedom

Members of THE PARTY OF PERSONAL FREEDOM support free markets. We defend the right of individuals to form corporations, cooperatives and other types of entities based on voluntary association. We oppose all forms of government subsidies and bailouts to business, labor, or any other special interest. Government should not compete with private enterprise.

2.7 Labor Markets

Employment and compensation agreements between private employers and employees are outside the scope of government, and these contracts should not be encumbered by government-mandated benefits or social engineering. We support the right of private employers and employees to choose whether or not to bargain with each other through a labor union. Bargaining should be free of government interference, such as compulsory arbitration or imposing an obligation to bargain. We oppose the compulsory payment of union dues by any employee who elects to not participate in a union.

2.8 Education

Education is best provided by the free market, achieving greater quality, accountability and efficiency with more diversity of choice. Recognizing that the education of children is a parental responsibility, we would restore authority to parents to determine the education of their children, without interference from government. Parents should have control of and responsibility for all funds expended for their children's education.

2.9 Healthcare

We favor a free market healthcare system. We recognize the freedom of individuals to determine the level of health insurance they want (if any), the level of healthcare they want, the care providers they want, the medicines and treatments they will use and all other aspects of their medical care, including end-of-life decisions. People should be free to purchase health insurance across state lines.

2.10 Retirement and Income Security

Retirement planning is the responsibility of the individual, not the government. Members of THE PARTY OF PERSONAL FREEDOM would phase out the current government-sponsored Social Security system and transition to a private voluntary system consisting of personally held 401-Ks and Individual Retirement Accounts. The proper and most effective source of help for the poor is the voluntary efforts of private groups and individuals. We believe members of society will become more charitable and civil society will be strengthened as government reduces its activity in this realm.

3.0 Securing Liberty

The protection of the country as a whole (national defense) and the protection of each individual's rights is the only proper purpose of government.

Government is constitutionally limited so as to prevent the infringement of individual rights by the government itself. The principle of non-initiation of force should guide the relationships between governments.

3.1 National Defense

We support the maintenance of a sufficient military to defend the United States against aggression. The United States should use discretion when entering into international alliances and abandon its attempts to act as policeman for the world. We oppose any form of compulsory national service.

3.2 Internal Security and Individual Rights

The defense of the country requires that we have adequate intelligence to detect and to counter threats to domestic security. This requirement must not take priority over maintaining the civil liberties of our citizens. The Constitution and Bill of Rights shall not be suspended even during time of war. Intelligence agencies that legitimately seek to preserve the security of the nation must be subject to oversight and transparency. We oppose the government's use of secret classifications to keep from the public information that it should have, especially that which shows that the government has violated the law.

3.3 International Affairs

American foreign policy should seek an America at peace with the world. Our foreign policy should emphasize defense against attack from abroad and enhance the likelihood of peace by entering into mutual defense agreements with our country's allies. We recognize the right of all people to resist tyranny and defend themselves and their rights. We condemn the use of force, and especially the use of terrorism, against the innocent, regardless of whether such acts are committed by governments or by political or revolutionary groups.

3.4 Free Trade and Migration

We support the removal of governmental impediments to free trade. Economic freedom demands the movement of human as well as financial capital across national borders. However, our country must maintain secure borders, and we support strong controls over the entry into our country of foreign nationals who pose a credible threat to security, health or property. We welcome immigrants who come to our country legally in accordance with our country's immigration laws. We also support the ongoing efforts to address the issues surrounding people who have entered our country illegally, and we oppose the granting of citizenship to people who are not legal residents of our country.

3.5 Rights and Discrimination

Members of THE PARTY OF PERSONAL FREEDOM embrace the concept that all people are born with certain inherent rights. We reject the idea that a natural right can ever impose an obligation upon others to fulfill that "right." We condemn bigotry as irrational and repugnant. Government should neither deny nor abridge any individual's human right based upon sex, wealth, ethnicity, creed, age, national origin, personal habits, political preference or sexual orientation. Members of private organizations retain their rights to set whatever standards of association they deem appropriate, and individuals are free to respond with ostracism, boycotts and other free market solutions. Parents, or other guardians, have the right to raise their children according to their own standards and beliefs. This statement shall not be construed to condone child abuse or neglect.

3.6 Representative Government

We support election systems that are more representative of the electorate at the federal, state and local levels. As private voluntary groups, political parties should be allowed to establish their own rules for nomination procedures, primaries and conventions. We call for an end to any tax-financed subsidies to candidates or parties and the repeal of all laws which restrict voluntary financing of election campaigns. We oppose laws that effectively exclude alternative candidates and parties, deny ballot access, gerrymander districts, or deny the voters their right to consider all legitimate alternatives. We advocate initiative, referendum, recall and repeal when used as popular checks on government.

3.7 Self-Determination

Whenever any form of government becomes destructive of individual liberty, it is the right of the people to alter or to abolish it, and to agree to such new governance as to them shall seem most likely to protect their liberty.

4.0 Our Party's Priorities

4.1 Shrink the size and scope of the federal government

The members of THE PARTY OF PERSONAL FREEDOM support any and all changes that serve to reduce the size and scope of the federal government's activities, and help the government focus exclusively on its responsibilities that are listed in Article 1, Section 8 of the US Constitution. We seek to restore the concept behind the Tenth Amendment - - The powers not delegated to the United States by the Constitution, nor prohibited by it to the States, are reserved to the States respectively, or to the people.

4.2 Support and expand the role of Civil Society

Our members support changes to the country's income tax policies that serve to increase opportunity for all of the country's citizens, and we want to eliminate any provision of the current income tax code that provides favoritism towards any "special interest group" or sub-segment of the population.

The country's income tax policies should never be used to "socially engineer" the country's citizens. We want to restore the concept of Personal Responsibility, rather than create reliance upon a government program. We want to implement changes that enhance financial support to Not-for-Profit charities and other organizations that can help people take Personal Responsibility for their own lives.

4.3 Repay the country's cumulative debt

As noted above, our members support the passage of a "Balanced Budget Amendment". Our country needs to first eliminate irresponsible deficit spending, and then begin to run surpluses for a number of years that will allow our federal government to repay the cumulative debt.

4.4 Establish Term Limits for members of the US Senate and US House of Representatives

Our members support the passage of the proposed amendment to the US Constitution for Term Limits for US Senators and members of the US House of Representatives (see www.termlimits.org).

4.5 Re-write the federal income tax code for personal income tax returns

Our members support changes that will significantly simplify the federal income tax code for personal income tax returns. These income tax changes would be implemented at the same time as the changes for Social Security Reform, Healthcare Reform, and Welfare Reform. Additional details on these changes can be found on the website www.F2PPR.org in a document entitled *The 2020 Initiative*.

4.6 Transform Social Security into a means-tested welfare benefit

With the ongoing changes in the country's demographics, future generations of workers are not going to be able to save for their own personal retirement if they continue to be coerced into paying for the retirement benefits of previous generations. Having said that, our country must continue to honor the commitments that have been made to citizens who are currently receiving Social Security benefits. However, we must begin to transform the Social Security program (over a multi-year transition period) for people who are not yet retired. The transition plan should ensure that all citizens receive a return of the contributions they have paid into the Social Security system through the month of December 2019.

4.7 Enact Healthcare Reform, and make changes to healthcare taxes

Our members believe that providing for healthcare is a Personal Responsibility. Healthcare (and food and housing and etc.) should not be viewed as being a right that should be bestowed upon an individual by the federal government. However, our members also believe that no citizen should face death due to a lack of care for a remediable life-threatening condition.

4.8 Enact Welfare Reform

The real solution to the problem of poverty is to help those less fortunate become "unpoor". The federal government should cease all of its welfare programs that have been established over the years to combat poverty, because this is not a proper role of the federal government. These government programs have been ineffective and counter-productive, serve to diminish the concept of Personal Responsibility, and create a sense of dependency upon the government. The members of THE PARTY OF PERSONAL FREEDOM support changes to the federal income tax code that will serve to redirect financial support away from the federal government and towards civil society (families and Not-for-Profit charities and religious organizations) as a more effective way to combat poverty.

5.0 Omissions

Our silence about any other particular government law, regulation, ordinance, directive, edict, control, regulatory agency, activity, or machination should not be construed to imply approval.

Excerpts from the 2016 Republican Party Platform

We reaffirm the Constitution's fundamental principles: limited government, separation of powers, individual liberty, and the rule of law… The current Administration has exceeded its constitutional authority, brazenly and flagrantly violated the separation of powers, sought to divide America into groups and turn citizen against citizen…

Forty-eight Democratic senators, for instance, voted to amend the Bill of Rights to give government officials control over political speech… Limits on political speech serve only to protect the powerful and insulate incumbent officeholders…

Our national platform has repeatedly endorsed term limits for Member of Congress. In response, the GOP Leadership in 1996 brought to a vote, in both the House and Senate, a constitutional amendment. It failed to secure the necessary two-thirds vote in the House, where 80 percent of Republicans voted for it and 80 percent of Democrats voted against it. Every Senate Republican voted to allow a vote on term limits, but the Democrats killed it by a filibuster. …to advance a constitutional amendment for consideration by the states, we must expand the current Republican majorities in both chambers…

Much of what the federal government does can be improved, much should be replaced, and much needs to be done away with or returned to the states. It is long past time for just tinkering around the edges of a bloated and unresponsive bureaucratic state…

Unelected bureaucrats must be stopped from furthering the Democratic Party's political agenda through regulatory demands forced upon citizen and businesses beyond that which is required by law…

The Administration's demands have focused on significantly expanding government spending and benefits for its preferred groups, paid for by loans that our children and grandchildren will have to repay. This is the path to bankrupting the next generation…

Republican budgets will prioritize thrift over extravagance and put taxpayers first. We support the following test: Is a particular expenditure within the constitutional scope of the federal government? If not, stop it...

We reject the old maxim that Social Security is the "Third Rail" of American politics, deadly for anyone who would change it. The Democratic Party still treats it that way, even though everyone knows that its current course will lead to a financial and social disaster. Younger Americans have lost all faith in the program and expect little return for what they are paying into it...

Cronyism is inherent in the progressive vision of the administrative state. When government uses taxpayer funding and resources to give special advantages to private companies, it distorts the free market and erodes public trust in our political system. By enlarging the scope of government and placing enormous power in the hands of bureaucrats, it multiplies opportunities for corruption and favoritism...

The federal workforce is larger and more highly paid than ever. The taxpayers spend an average of $35,000 a year per employee on non-cash benefits, triple the average worker in the private sector...

The question is whether we are going to reinvigorate the private-sector institutions under citizen control or allow their continued erosion by the forces of centralized social planning. In that divide, the Republican Party stand with the people...

Two grave problems undermine the rule of law on the federal level: over-criminalization and over-federalization. Congress and federal agencies have increase the number of criminal offenses in the US Code from 3,000 in the early 1980s to more than 4,500 today. The power of career civil servants and political appointees to criminalize behavior is one of the worst violations of constitutional order perpetrated by the administrative state...

We have been fighting the War on Poverty for 50 years and poverty is winning. Our social safety net – about 80 separate means-tested programs costing over $1 trillion every year – is designed to help people born into or falling into poverty. It rarely lifts them out. Its apologists judge success by the amount of money spent to keep people in the system. That is a cruel measurement. Republicans propose to evaluate a poverty program by whether it actually reduces poverty and increases the personal independence of its participants...

Over-regulation of start-up enterprises, excessive licensing requirements, needless restrictions on formation of schools and day-care centers serving neighborhood families, and restrictions on providing public services in fields like transport close the opportunity door to all but a favored few. We will continue our fight for school choice until all parents can find good, safe schools for their children. To protect religious liberty we will ensure that faith-based institutions, especially those that are vital parts of under-served neighborhoods, do not face discrimination by government...

Education is much more than schooling. It is the whole range of activities by which families and communities transmit to a younger generation, not just knowledge and skills, but ethical and behavioral norms and traditions. It is the handing over of a cultural identity. That is why American education has, for the last several decades, been the focus of constant controversy, as centralizing forces from outside the family and community have sought to "remake" education in order to "remake" America. They have done immense damage....

Breaking the cycle of crime begins with the children of those who are prisoners. Deprived of a parent through no fault of their own, youngsters from these families should be a special concern of our schools, social services and religious institutions...

In solidarity with those who protect us we call for mandatory prison time for all assaults involving serious injury to law enforcement officers... The Republican Party must make clear in word and action that every human life matters...

Excerpts from the 2016 Democratic Party Platform

[The comments in brackets are courtesy of the F2PPR Editorial Board. Simply put, the Democratic Party's platform represents a "divisive" agenda. The central themes of the platform are "fairness" and "equality" (which are good "sound bites", but there is no discussion about what those terms mean). The platform pits the interests of various special interest groups against the interests of other citizens. The various planks represent "Opportunities for Certain Select Special Interest Groups" and "Favoritism to that Special Interest Group", rather than policies that promote the general welfare of the country as a whole. The following is an excerpt from the platform's Table of Contents that lists the various initiatives and priorities, all of which are beyond the scope of the federal government's responsibilities that are listed in the US Constitution.]

Table of Contents –
Raising Workers' Wages [via government fiat, rather than in the context of the (global) marketplace]
Supporting Working Families [i.e., buying votes with other people's money]
Helping More Workers Share in Near-record Corporate Profits [i.e., Socialism - This plank ignores / excludes any discussion about the concepts of ownership, risk taking, and return on capital]
Expanding Access to Affordable Housing and Homeownership [Re-creating the housing bubble]
Protecting and Expanding Social Security [... at the expense of future generations]
Ensuring a Secure & Dignified Retirement [Isn't providing for retirement a Personal Responsibility?]
Revitalizing our Nation's Postal Service [The post office should be privatized instead]
Creating Good-paying Jobs [This is the role of the marketplace. The federal government cannot "create" good-paying jobs, except in the government sector - and who pays for those jobs??]
Supporting America's Small Businesses [Why not support all businesses by reducing taxes and government regulations?]

Creating Jobs for America's Young People [This is the role of the marketplace and civil society. Also, this will be much more difficult to accomplish if the government raises the minimum wage]

Fight for Economic Fairness and Against Inequality [...by using the Left's definition of "Fairness". The only way to truly eliminate inequality is to implement Communism]

Promoting Competition by Stopping Corporate Concentration [Is this the role of government? Also, interestingly, the best paying jobs in America are oftentimes paid by larger businesses]

Making the Wealthy Pay Their Fair Share of Taxes [...by using the Left's definition of "Fairness"]

Promoting Trade that is Fair and Benefits American Workers [...by using the Left's definition of "Fairness". This oftentimes pits American workers against consumers (who are the same people)]

Investing in Rural America
Building Strong Cities and Metro Areas
Promoting Arts and Culture
Fighting for the People of Puerto Rico
Build a Clean Energy Economy
Secure Environmental Justice
Provide Quality and Affordable Education
Making Debt-free College a Reality
Providing Relief from Crushing Student Debt
Ensure the Health and Safety of All Americans
Securing Universal Health Care
Reducing Prescription Drug Costs
Treating Mental Health [Is this really a role for the federal government ?]
Supporting Those Living with Autism and their Families
Securing Reproductive Health, Rights, and Justice
Ensuring Long-Term Care, Services, and Supports [...with other people's money]
[Etc., Etc. - - There really is no end to the progressive agenda]

[Each of the programs listed above represent an attempt by the Left to put into place the policies and programs of federal government "experts". This will be accomplished at the expense of the marketplace and civil society (families, Not-for-Profit charitable organizations, religious institutions, and other local "communities"). It is readily apparent that with the advance of the liberal / progressive agenda, civil society will have a vastly reduced role to play, because the federal government needs to become the most powerful force in people's lives.

With each new program put forward by the federal government, the concepts of Personal Responsibility and individual liberty are diminished.

We suspect that most of the initiatives listed above have (probably) been put forward with the best of intentions. However, these initiatives also represent an attempt to buy people's votes. Many of these programs are being put forward without consideration of any possible "unintended consequences" and/or without regard to an analysis of costs versus benefits. Do we really want to have the federal government exercise that much control over the marketplace and our day to day lives?

Please refer to the Seven Inevitable Results that were listed in the August newsletter.]

Healthcare Re-Visited

Listen to your mother, and eat your vegetables. If you smoke, quit. Get at least a half hour of moderately strenuous exercise several times a week. Don't do drugs / Just say no. But be sure to take your medication(s) prescribed by your doctor. Try to get the recommended amount of sleep each night. If you're overweight, try to lose some of those extra pounds....

OK... Now that we have re-established the fact that healthcare is a Personal Responsibility, let's move on to the unresolved issue of who should pay for an individual's / family's health insurance policy. Unfortunately, the Socialists of the Left have commingled the issue of "healthcare" with the issue of acquiring health insurance. So the purpose of this conversation piece is to focus on the issues regarding health insurance. On our website, we have an October 2013 Conversation Piece entitled *Medicare and Universal Health Care Coverage*, where we discuss the concepts of insurance, and make some comparisons /

contrasts between health insurance and other types of insurance, like auto insurance. We are going to set aside the issues relating to Medicare, and focus on health insurance for individuals / families prior to retirement.

Our Editorial Board continues to believe that the cost of health insurance (similar to the cost of food, housing, auto insurance, education, etc.) is a Personal Responsibility. Bernie Sanders believes that healthcare is somehow different, that healthcare is a "right", and that the cost of health insurance should somehow become a responsibility of the federal government. We couldn't disagree more. As we noted in our previous Conversation Piece, the federal government (via the "individual mandate" that was created in 2010) believes that the cost of health insurance should be treated like a "tax". And unfortunately, the Supreme Court subsequently agreed. But the good news is that this over-reach by the federal government can be overturned by repealing the (Un)Affordable Care Act. The debate about the repeal of Obamacare is not a debate about "healthcare" - - it is a debate about who pays for whose health insurance premiums.

Our Editorial Board believes that health insurance is simply insurance, and is just another commodity in the marketplace. Doctor fees, hospital bills, prescription drugs, and other healthcare expenses are also simply commodities in the marketplace. Having said that... We do agree that because of the possibility of severe financial repercussions that could arise due to a serious illness or injury, a person would be exercising prudent Personal Responsibility by acquiring a health insurance policy.

The current debate is driven by the fact that health insurance is expensive. And one of the fundamental questions that needs to be addressed is "Why is that?" The answer to that question (to a large degree) is due to the distortions in the marketplace that have been caused by the federal government. We will get to Obamacare in a moment, but we first need to go back further in time to the 1940s and 1950s.

Prior to World War II, few citizens had health insurance. And if they did, most policies covered only hospital costs and ancillary services. During WW II, when wages were frozen by the National War Labor Board and there was a shortage of workers, employers sought out different ways to get around the wage controls in order to attract scarce workers. Offering health insurance was one solution.

That approach, by itself, would have been OK. The marketplace adapts to issues that arise in the marketplace. However, the federal government thought that it would "help out" by making changes to the country's tax laws. The

102

Revenue Act of 1954 included a provision whereby the cost of an employer's contribution to a health insurance plan was excluded in determining an employee's taxable income. Interestingly, this is probably the only instance within the entire US tax code where one party (the employer) can take a tax deduction, and the related counterparty (the employee) does not need to report the income. It certainly is one of the largest "tax preference" items in the tax code. The cost of this tax preference item is estimated to be approximately $275 billion per year in foregone tax revenues (which then needs to be financed by the government via other taxes and/or increases in the national debt).

One of the other "unintended consequences" that occurred because of this change in the tax code is that employees have never truly understood the cost of this health insurance benefit. Unfortunately however, entrepreneurs and other self-employed individuals are painfully aware of the cost of health insurance.

Another effect is that employees have been shielded from understanding the true cost of their own personal healthcare decisions, because of the low out of pocket costs and deductibles that are available under some of these group health insurance plans. And when there is no self-imposed check on the demand for healthcare services, there is an upward effect on prices. (And we don't even want to get into a discussion about the number of hypochondriacs this federal tax policy may have created over the years).

So, rather than learn from our past mistakes about the distortions in the marketplace that are caused by the federal government, our elected representatives decided that the federal government should further intrude into the marketplace by passing the (Un)Affordable Care Act.

And what have we learned? Between 2013 and 2017, within the marketplace for individual health insurance policies, twenty-four states have seen premiums more than double. And in three states, the premiums have more than tripled. For 2018, insurers are announcing additional huge rate increases, and many insurers are simply withdrawing from the various state insurance exchanges. Similarly, the costs for group health insurance plans have also skyrocketed, primarily due to the "employer mandates" that were embedded in this disastrous legislation.

Please keep in mind that Obamacare was put forward with the best of intentions - to make health insurance "more affordable" – but this is something that the federal government cannot accomplish. Obamacare is collapsing because it should never have been implemented in the first place, and all of the additional regulations and mandates that were created by this legislation should be repealed.

So, what should the replacement be? Before we get into a discussion about our recommendations, let's re-visit a few fundamental questions. Why should health insurance be any different than any other type of insurance? Why should employers be caught up in the procurement and administration of a group health insurance program? (Shouldn't they be focusing on their business)? Why isn't health insurance "portable" from one job to the next? Why shouldn't health insurance policies be individually owned, like auto insurance or homeowners insurance? Why can't health insurance be sold by insurance companies across state line? Why is health insurance the only situation in the US tax code, where an employer gets to deduct a cost, and the employee doesn't need to report the income? Why do "employees" get a tax advantage that is not available to self-employed people?

Our Editorial Board's recommendations are as follows. These recommendations pertain to the 85% of the country's population who have been adversely affected by Obamacare. We will then wrap up with a discussion about the 45 million people who didn't have health insurance prior to Obamacare. And there are still approximately 25-30 million people who do not, seven years later.

Employers should continue to sponsor group health insurance plans, if such plans serve as an effective recruiting / retention tool within their market. And they can continue to assist employees in acquiring an affordable health insurance policy that best meets an employee's needs. However, individual employees should be able to more easily acquire a health insurance policy that is individually owned, and therefore portable from one job to the next. Any employer cost for a health insurance program should be treated as taxable compensation to the employee, leveling the playing field between employees and self-employed individuals.

Health Savings Accounts should be available for all individuals / families. HSAs can be arranged through your employer, or can be set up individually. Any otherwise taxable income that is personally set aside in an HSA during the year should be excluded from the determination of taxable income. These funds are personally owned money (personally saved money) that can be used to pay for health insurance premiums or any other type of qualified healthcare expense.

Here is an insurance "choice" issue that can best be described by making a comparison to auto insurance. Although "auto repair and maintenance" insurance policies exist, very few people buy these (expensive) policies that pay the cost of repair bills. Instead, consumers tend to buy an auto insurance policy (for a much lower premium) that primarily covers the exposure to catastrophic losses. Similarly, individuals / families should consider buying a high deductible (catastrophic loss coverage) health insurance policy. If they buy this type of policy when they are young (and maintain continuous coverage), they can retain the difference in premium costs within their own personally-owned Health Savings Account, which can then be used to cover the cost of routine healthcare expenses.

Once a personally-owned high deductible insurance policy has been obtained and continuous coverage has been maintained, an individual / family should be shielded from "changes in conditions". In regards to "pre-existing conditions"... If a young adult comes off of their parent's health insurance policy with a pre-existing condition and their coverage had been maintained by their parents, they should not be penalized in the marketplace by that insurance company when they go to acquire their own individually-owned policy.

So, what happens if you do have a pre-existing condition and/or you haven't maintained continuous coverage - - how do you get back into the insurance market? The "easiest" way would be to find an employer who can get you covered under their group health insurance program. Once coverage has been established and then continuously maintained, you should be able to subsequently move to an individually-owned high deductible insurance policy, if that best meets your needs. Again, the most important element of the above recommendations is to set aside as much money as possible in an HSA to cover the cost of health insurance premiums and other healthcare costs.

So, that leaves us with the question of what can be done for low-income individuals / families who find it difficult to afford a health insurance policy (or set aside funds in an HSA). On our website, we have a June 2016 Conversation Piece entitled *The 2020 Initiative*. In a few months, we will post a new Conversation Piece entitled *Welfare Reform Re-Visited*. In that piece, we will discuss how the real solution to the problem of poverty in America is to help those less fortunate become "unpoor".

One of the key features of *The 2020 Initiative* is a change to the US tax code for personal income taxes, whereby charitable contributions to various "pre-approved" Not-for-Profit charities will result in a tax credit against an individual's / family's federal income tax liability that would otherwise be paid into the swamp. The federal government needs to be starved of these funds, so that it no longer intrudes into the marketplace for healthcare, housing, education, etc., or any other arena that is not specifically identified in the US Constitution as being a responsibility of the federal government.

In *The 2020 Initiative*, we recommend that four national Not-for-Profit "clearing-house charities" be established for food, housing, healthcare and education. The sole purpose of these national charities is to collect funds from citizens, and then, based on stringent, objective criteria that quantifies each state's needs, disburse that charity's funds to the applicable state-level charitable organization in each state. We also recommend that a state's citizens' payroll tax withholdings for healthcare be immediately remitted back to that same state-level charitable healthcare organization.

As we will discuss in our upcoming Conversation Piece on *Welfare Reform Re-Visited*, the better solution is to have the people who need assistance rely on civil society, rather than the federal government, to meet their needs. It will be up to the states, and that state's local charities and local community organizations to efficiently manage the use of these funds. The state-level Medicaid program, working with that state's local charities, "free clinics", and other local community groups will have the primary responsibility for the delivery of healthcare services to those individuals / families, who need to participate in this public-sector healthcare solution, until that point in time when those citizens can begin to participate in the private-sector healthcare market.

Welfare Reform Re-Visited

Warning: The following assertion / recommendation is probably going to cause severe distress to anyone who is of a liberal/progressive persuasion or who might have "Democratic Socialism" tendencies.... No governmental unit (at the federal, state or local level) should ever provide a cash payment (or a cash-like benefit, such as food stamps) to any citizen. Ever. We don't believe that governments, charities, or social services agencies should ever give cash to a citizen - - goods and services are OK. Only families or a local community group should give cash to a person in need.

The reasoning here is fairly straightforward. Cash given to a citizen by the government (unless it is a substantial and permanently re-occurring amount, and only a Socialist would ever consider such an approach) can only serve to marginally and temporarily make that person somewhat less poor. Cash payments from the government do not provide a solution to poverty. What's worse is that the detrimental

effects of this approach are even more insidious - - Cash received from the government
only serves to increase the sense of entitlement among our country's citizens,
and increases the recipient's dependency on government. This is a simple fact,
and cannot be refuted by the Socialists of the Left. Unfortunately,
"entitlement" and dependency (along with a bigger, more intrusive federal
government) appear to be the ultimate goals of the progressive movement.
Unfortunately, the Left likes to advertise the dollar amount of "entitlements"
and welfare benefits that the government doles out each year. This is a
perverse measurement of "success".

And here is a recommendation that is probably even more distressing to those on the Left
- - No governmental unit (at the federal, state or local level) should ever attempt to
administer a welfare program. Ever.

Thomas Paine, in his pamphlet entitled **Common Sense**, made the following observation –
*Some writers have so confounded society with government, as to leave little or no
distinction between them; whereas they are not only different, but have different
origins. Society is produced by our want, and government by our wickedness; the
former promotes our happiness POSITIVELY by uniting our affections, the latter
NEGATIVELY by restraining our vices.... Society in every state is a blessing, but
Government, even in its best state, is but a necessary evil; in its worst state an
intolerable one.*

Thomas Jefferson put it this way – *If we can but prevent the government from wasting
the labours of the people, under the pretence of taking care of them, they must become
happy.*

So, the real question is… When did the progressives begin to lose their
Common Sense? Or maybe the better question would be… Did they ever have
any Common Sense? Why would anyone ever think that the government
could be a benevolent entity? We believe that it's safe to say that this collective
loss of Common Sense began to happen well before 1935, however, it became
institutionalized with the start of the Social Security program.

As we noted above, this Conversation Piece is not going to be received very
well by supporters of the current welfare state's status quo. In fact, this Piece
is our Foundation's attempt to "terminate" both "Sugar Daddy" and the "Fairy
Godmother", and cause some serious damage to the concept of a benevolent
"Big Brother".

In **The 2020 Initiative**, we simply advocate the resurrection of civil society.
Over the past 100 years or so, the federal government has gradually usurped
the role of civil society and has stolen (via coercive taxation) the funds that

would otherwise have gone to charities and other local community groups and social service agencies – the very groups that have been established by civil society to provide support to people in need. There is no doubt that people living in poverty need goods and (more importantly) services to help escape poverty. In **The 2020 Initiative**, we recommend the creation of four "pass-through" national charities, which would be funded by We-the-People, who would be allowed to divert a portion of their federal income taxes to one or more of these charities, instead of continuing to send all of their tax dollars into the federal government swamp.

Let's start with Education. The country's public education system is in decline / failing. It is time to get the government out of education and return it to the local community - - to the parents, the local school's teachers, and the local Parent Teacher Association. We need to fix the K-12 education system, and shrink the local school's administrative costs, by eliminating the wasted time and effort that are spent on complying with the requirements of the Administrative State.

And unfortunately, because of the current sorry state of K-12 public education, there is a critical need for all kinds of remedial education services, including job training programs for people who are already out of high school. This will require a large amount of funding to local community groups to provide these remedial education and job training services. Our recommendation is to direct those funds toward local community "junior college" job training programs. This approach does not give a cash welfare payment to people in need; instead this solution is based on providing a vital service to those people who will take their own initiative to lift themselves out of poverty.

Let's move on to Food, which is a basic fundamental need. We recommend local food banks (probably at least one food bank in each county in every state) that would provide these goods to local citizens in need. This welfare program would discontinue the approach of providing cash and/or food stamps, but instead would rely upon charitable contributions from civil society to fund the operation of these local food banks. And this solution would harness the best logistics / distribution technologies, along with the buying power of bulk purchases of generic, healthful items, to provide life's most basic necessities at the most efficient, cost-effective price. Compassionate citizens of all political persuasions would support the idea that these goods (not cash) be provided to someone in need as long as necessary, until the recipient has been able to lift his-/herself out of poverty. But there should be a counter-requirement for this welfare benefit - - the recipient would need to be simultaneously executing their own education / employment game plan to accomplish the goal of lifting his-/herself out of a poverty level existence.

Housing? Again, another fundamental need. Every person needs a safe and secure residence - a place that gives shelter from the weather / the elements, and provides a safe environment for that individual / family. We see two types of assistance that the local community needs to be able to provide. We recommend that this good (a shelter) and service (publicly provided shelter, utilities and a connection to the internet) be provided by a local Habitat for Humanity social services agency in each county in every state. In the first type of instance, the immediate, short term solution would be a "tiny house." These shelters would be owned by the agency, would be "mobile" as needed, would be re-usable, and would be used to meet an immediate need for a safe place for someone who has been displaced by domestic violence, or a traumatic circumstance (such as fire or flooding), or eviction. We see the local Habitat for Humanity agency partnering with the American Red Cross (or a similar charitable organization) in those circumstances that require a larger relief effort. But this type of temporary, short term solution would need to be bolstered by a longer-term strategy for the recipient(s) of this service.

A recipient's longer-term situation will require a longer-term, more permanent solution. The cost of housing is a challenge for low income citizens. For people in the lowest quintile of income (the lowest 20%) the cost of housing consumes nearly 60% of their income. (For the other 80% of the country's population, the cost of housing consumes between 22-27% of their income). We reject the idea of giving a welfare recipient a cash payment that can be used towards housing. We also reject the concept of large-scale public housing - - that approach has already been tried by the government in the past and has failed miserably. What our Editorial Board recommends is a "rent to own" solution. Habitat for Humanity groups have proven to be very effective in building / rehabilitating single family homes. But before a welfare recipient could participate in this longer-term solution, they would need to have developed and begun to execute a viable game plan geared towards emerging from a poverty level existence. The successful execution of the first steps in this game-plan would make them eligible to move out of the "tiny house" solution and into the "rent to own" solution.

Healthcare. See our Conversation Piece on **Healthcare Re-Visited**. The federal government needs to get out of the business of trying to manage the country's healthcare system. The free market is always a better solution, and will provide the best, most cost-effective solution (to the 85% of the country's population who are not in poverty). For those people who do require assistance, there should be a state/local-level "public" option available to people in need. These "free" (or discounted) health clinics would be funded by civil society, and would deliver "below market cost" services to welfare-eligible recipients. As we noted in **The 2020 Initiative**, one of the key cost saving features that would need to be implemented in connection with this "public" healthcare option is that recipients of these free/discounted services would be precluded from filing litigation claims against the agencies and providers of these public healthcare services. We anticipate that a lot of these free/discounted services would be provided by local civic-minded volunteers.

As we have noted above, the over-riding goal of **The 2020 Initiative** is to remove the federal government's involvement from those day to day activities that represent an individual's Personal Responsibility. Career politicians would no longer be able to bribe our country's citizens with our own money (or in the case of annual deficits and debt, our children's and grandkids' money). The federal government has enough on its plate, and it has a big enough role to play, with just discharging (effectively) its responsibilities that are listed in the Constitution.

OK, now this is going to sound "unfeeling" and overly harsh.... But one additional problem that the federal government has caused over the past 100 years or so, is that it has attempted to "de-stigmatize" dependency. A century ago, our country's citizens had a well-grounded aversion to being on the dole. Unfortunately, one of the Left's primary goals has been to eliminate this stigma. And with all of the government "entitlements" that are available, many of our citizens have begun to feel that they are entitled to receive a wide variety of "free stuff" from the government. Fortunately, most people understand economics and the fact that there is no such thing as a free lunch.

Another problem is in regards to the way the US tax code is administered - - If your income is too low, you don't need to file an annual income tax return. This doesn't mean that the federal government doesn't already get a portion of your wages (which is OK). Our Editorial Board believes that until the "entitlement" mess that was created by Social Security and Medicare has been fixed, every citizen should contribute 10% of their annual W-2 taxable wages via payroll tax withholdings. This is simply every citizen's obligation and contribution towards digging ourselves out of the collective hole that has been dug. But having said that... Our Editorial Board feels that these wages should only be taxed once, and no individual / family should ever have to pay "federal income taxes" until they have earned enough taxable income to surpass the applicable federal poverty guideline amount.

Another key feature of **The 2020 Initiative** is that before any citizen could expect to receive goods and/or services from a local Not for Profit social services agency, they would need to "request" such assistance each year on their federal income tax return. This annual tax return process would also serve as an annual "financial check-up" to see if that individual / family is making progress on their journey out of poverty. Unfortunately, under the current rules where an annual tax return is not required, this has probably served to foster a feeling of "What's the point? I am a victim. I am not a participant in our country's economy. I am just along for the ride."

Lastly, our Editorial Board would like to see the Social Security Administration transformed into a useful, productive government agency - - an "information clearing house" that would be available to individuals / families in need. If we could transform the Social Security program into being a means-tested welfare benefit, these civil servants in the Social Security Administration could be re-trained to become counselors to welfare recipients, and provide information on where those individuals can go to receive the appropriate goods and services they need, in order to help them address their own specific situation. Social Security agents could become consultants who could work with these individuals / families on developing a life plan that will enable them to become "unpoor".

Now, that would be a better solution to the issue of poverty, rather than simply dispensing cash "entitlements" to people.

Other Thoughts on Personal Responsibility

In our February 2016 newsletter, we included a link to a five-minute video that highlights the fundamental difference between the Left and the Right in regards to their views on the role and size of the government. The video discusses seven "Inevitable Results of Big Government", and we recommend that everyone re-visit those seven self-evident truths –

https://www.prageru.com/courses/left-and-right-differences/how-big-should-government-be-left-vs-right-1

-   -   -   -   -

One of the tactics used by the Socialists of the Left to increase the size and scope of the federal government is to promote the concept of victimization. As we noted in our very first Conversation Piece entitled *Why Mitt Romney's Comments About the 47% Were Not Correct*, we acknowledge that some people are truly victims (of crimes and accidents). Conservatives believe that in those situations, it is up to family members and civil society groups (not the federal government) to help those victims after they have been victimized. Unfortunately, many on the Left try to expand the definition of "victims" by promoting the concept of "victims of circumstances". The Left then demands that the federal government solve each of these victims' problem(s). And then, while the government is at it, go ahead and use the coercive power of the government (taxation) to solve a perplexing (to them) "social ill", because they feel the government has a responsibility to eliminate inequality.

The Left does not believe in Personal Responsibility (they would prefer to establish yet another government program). We agree that it is probably true that the Left agrees with the concept of Opportunity for All as it relates to protecting citizens' rights. However, the Socialists' definition of Opportunity for All includes the concept of taxing middle class and wealthy individuals, so that those citizens' wealth can be redistributed to eliminate "economic inequality".

-    -   -   -   -

Our country's Founders were well aware of the detrimental effects on society that would result from the growth in size and scope (and intrusiveness) of the federal government. Accordingly, the Tenth Amendment states – *The powers not delegated to the United States by the Constitution, nor prohibited by it to the States, are reserved to the States respectively, **or to the people*** [emphasis added].

-    -   -   -   -

Our Editorial Board believes that every US citizen should be subject to a minimal amount of Personal Financial Responsibility to our federal government, which was established by the States to militarily defend the country as a whole, and protect the rights of our country's citizens. Until we can dig ourselves out of our collective $20 trillion hole (which is largely due to the Socialist programs entitled Social Security, Medicare and Medicaid) we feel that every citizen should contribute 10% of their wage income towards their financial obligation to the federal government. Having said that... These wages should only be taxed once, and no individual / family should pay any more than this 10% amount, until their annual taxable income begins to exceed the applicable federal poverty guideline amount. We also believe that every individual / family should have a Personal Responsibility to file an annual federal income tax return (which should be much simpler than the incomprehensible tax form that currently exists). And we believe that any individual /family who feels they need assistance should be required to substantiate their ongoing need(s) each year, and should work with the applicable government agencies and civil society groups to develop their own life plan to escape poverty.

- - - - -

Our Editorial Board believes that every citizen should have a sense of Personal Responsibility to vote in every local, state and federal election. We live in a society that utilizes a representative form of government at the local, state, and federal levels. These governmental units have been established to promote the general welfare of the citizenry as a whole. This form of self-government was established with the intent that each citizen would become engaged enough in the democratic process to educate themselves, in order to form opinions and be able to select between competing ideologies and platforms. We do not expect citizens to micro-manage the execution of governmental functions; this is the reason why we have a representative form of government at all three levels. We have all heard the saying that a person really doesn't have a right to complain about "the government" (local, state or federal) if they choose not to vote. We agree.

- - - - -

If you truly believe in the concepts of Personal Responsibility and Liberty, and understand the fundamental differences between the roles of civil society versus government (i.e., Common Sense), you would support the idea that the federal government should not be involved (at all) in education, food, housing, healthcare, or any type of welfare program, or any type of program that pays out unfunded pension benefits to retirees.

- - - - -

*We hold these truths to be self-evident, that all men are created equal, that they are endowed by their Creator with certain unalienable rights, that among these are life, liberty and the pursuit of happiness. That to secure these rights, governments are instituted among men, deriving their just powers from the consent of the governed. That whenever any form of government becomes destructive to these ends, it is the right of the people **to alter or to abolish** it, and to institute new government, laying its foundation on such principles and organizing its powers in such form, as to them shall seem most likely to effect their safety and happiness....*

Our Editorial Board believes that because of the detrimental effects that have been caused by the liberal/progressive movement, each one of us has a Personal Responsibility to halt and then begin to reverse the Socialistic trends that have occurred over the past 100 years. We need to re-institute the fundamental, foundational principles that were established by the Founders to ensure our citizens' safety and happiness. As we have noted on our Foundation's website, we do not see a need to abolish the current form of government. However, we do see an obvious need to make the following alterations -

To implement Term Limits for members of the US House of Representatives and the US Senate,

To re-establish fiscal responsibility within our federal government, and

To end crony capitalism and continue to combat the scourge of Socialism

We believe the time has come for 34 states to move forward and pass the necessary legislation that would call for a Convention of States under Article V of the Constitution. The purpose of such a convention would be to propose amendments to the US Constitution to impose fiscal restraints on the federal government, limit the power and jurisdiction of the federal government, and limit the terms of office for its officials and for members of Congress. We encourage every citizen to visit the website *www.conventionofstates.com* to learn more about Article V, which was the "fail safe" mechanism given to us by the Founders in the Constitution to check the powers of the federal government.

- - - - -

Our Editorial Board would like to see the Social Security Administration transformed into a more useful, productive government agency. The SSA should move away from being a "dispenser of cash benefits" and become an organization that has the responsibility to make an annual determination of an individual's / family's eligibility for welfare benefits. The SSA should be transformed into an agency that helps direct people in need towards the appropriate charities and local social services agencies that can best help that individual / family. Ultimately, ideally, the SSA should become an agency that provides consultation and coaching to actually assist those citizens on their journey towards Personal Responsibility and financial independence – the best way to escape poverty.

- - - - -

The increase in people's longevity (which is a good thing) has been one of the major factors why businesses in the private sector have curtailed pension plans. The result has been to shift the Personal Responsibility for providing for your own retirement to the individual. So... Question: The same increase in life expectancy is also true for employees in the public sector, so why doesn't the government sector operate under the same set of economic/demographic rules? And here is a more important set of questions: Why do we have career politicians? And why should any elected official (who should only hold an office for a limited number of years) be paid a government pension? And shouldn't they be responsible to save for their own retirement like everyone else?

- - - - -

Regarding retirement and healthcare... The beauty of Individual Retirement Accounts and 401-K plans is that you get a double benefit. The (otherwise) taxable income that you receive can be set aside and is not currently taxable, and any subsequent investment earnings that are credited to your IRA / 401-K account are also not taxed. You only pay taxes later in life when you start to draw down on the funds after you have retired (and are probably in a lower tax bracket).

Health Savings Accounts provide you with a triple benefit. Similar to retirement accounts, any of your personal funds that you set aside, along with the investment earnings in your HSA, escape taxation. The third benefit is that once you use these funds for qualified medical expenses, those funds are never subject to federal income taxes. Congress finally got one thing right. This is one of the best ways for you to assume Personal Responsibility for your own healthcare expenses.

- - - - -

Regarding public housing / welfare.... A key component of the American dream for most people has always included the idea of owning your own home. Granted, some people prefer to rent, but we believe that, given a choice, most people would enjoy the Personal Responsibility of owning their own home. Our proposed solution to the issue of housing is geared towards individual, private ownership of your own home, and rejects the idea of "public housing" and housing vouchers.

- - - - -

Regarding education.... Our Editorial Board believes in the concept of Opportunity for All. But this also means that each individual needs to assume the Personal Responsibility for figuring out the type of life that they would like to pursue - - whether that means becoming the CEO of a company, the President of the United States, or living off the grid in Alaska. And it is up to civil society (i.e., families, and not the faceless federal government) to assist each individual as they develop their life skills and begin to build the life that they want to pursue. Our Editorial Board supports the concept of School Choice, and we believe in the power of families, supported by local community groups and the local PTA, to help make that happen.

-    -   -   -   -

Regarding food... Each of us needs to be Personally Responsible for getting our own daily bread.

Other Musings

Regarding Liberty and the Bill of Rights and the Freedom of Speech.... The Left's ideology and their definition of "acceptable politically correct speech" run roughshod over the individual. This attack on individual Liberty is ultimately extremely dangerous. Our Editorial Board believes in our citizens' unfettered right to free speech. This includes those situations where the expression of controversial views (even by the lunatic fringe of either the Left or the Right) is abhorrent to the vast majority of everyone else in civil society.

Sticks and stones my break my bones, but words will never hurt me. It is true that "hate speech" (by its very definition) is hateful. However, every individual is free to make their own decisions in life, and develop their own set of values. Your rejection of speech that you deem to be hateful can even serve to strengthen your own set of values. Every citizen should be concerned about any limitations on our First Amendment rights, because the next attack on "hate speech" might be defined by (and might be carried out by) someone with a different viewpoint, and it might be directed towards eliminating one of your own personal values.

-    -   -

If angels were to govern men, neither external nor internal controls on government would be necessary. In framing a government which is to be administered by men over men, the great difficulty lies in this: you must first enable the government to control the governed; and in the next place oblige it to control itself. - James Madison, in The Federalist # 51

Unfortunately, men are not angels, and history includes innumerable examples of where political power plus money (especially when it's someone else's money) has led to corruption.

\- - -

Also unfortunately, there is plenty of "private" money (from both the Left and the Right) that is sloshing around in the swamp. Special interests and crony capitalism abound within the swamp. And then there are the career politicians who do not have any qualms about using our citizens' own tax dollars to buy votes by bribing the citizenry with our own tax dollars.

An avaricious man might be tempted to betray the interest of the state for the acquisition of wealth. - Alexander Hamilton

\- - -

Inflation is a tax on the prudent, who have to stand by and watch the value of their bank accounts and bond investments magically disappear. Inflation is a subsidy for scam artists who can borrow money for harebrained schemes and pay it back later with money that has no value. And inflation is a hardship for the old and the poor, who live on fixed incomes. Government deficits are well-hidden from the public and are less immediately painful than high inflation or huge tax increases, although constantly re-occurring deficits eventually lead to both.

\- - -

Over the past 50-60 years or so, the federal government's elites and its "experts" have attempted to "socially engineer" our country's citizens via manipulations and changes to the US tax code. This is part of the reason why the US tax code is now over 74,000 pages long. Our Editorial Board believes that it is time for We-the-People to begin to socially re-engineer the federal government, and divert funds away from the federal government and towards Not-for-Profit charities and other local community groups that can actually help those people who are in need, so that those individuals / families can lift themselves out of poverty.

\- - -

It will be of little avail to the people, that the laws are made by men of their own choice, if the laws be so voluminous that they cannot be read, or so incoherent that they cannot be understood. – Alexander Hamilton

It is time to "socially re-engineer" the federal government, and begin dismantling the Administrative State by eliminating all counter-productive regulations that have been implemented over the years.

-    -   -

The reason why our Editorial Board characterizes *The 2020 Initiative* as being a "nonpartisan" solution to help correct the country's growing debt problem is that it includes provisions that run counter to the tenets of both political parties. In other words, it will take bipartisan compromise to implement the recommendations that are included in *The 2020 Initiative*.

The Right needs to acknowledge that wealthy individuals will need to continue to be the primary source of funds for both the operation of the federal government and for civil society. The Left needs to acknowledge that each citizen needs to take Personal Responsibility for their own life. Although our Editorial Board agrees that reducing the size and scope of the federal government and the level of taxation would most definitely have a positive effect on the economy's growth rate, we do not feel that tax revenues should be decreased (yet) until the year that the federal government's annual deficit has been eliminated. And although we support the concept of a flat tax rate that should be applied at the same rate on the taxable income for all citizens, the majority of our Editorial Board agrees that progressive tax rates will need to remain in place until the federal government has begun to repay the cumulative debt. And we also mostly agree that the "death tax" (aka the estate tax) should not be repealed until the federal government's cumulative debt has been repaid.

The Left needs to give up its tactic of buying people's votes with other people's money. The Left also needs to disavow Socialism and Big Government, and agree that the federal government should focus **only** on those responsibilities that are listed in the US Constitution. This means that we need to correct the fundamental flaws of Social Security and other welfare programs, eliminate these programs from federal government spending, and rely upon civil society to take care of people who are in need of assistance. It is time to dismantle the Administrative State and allow civil society to re-establish itself. Charitable contributions will naturally flow to those social service agencies and local community groups that prove to be the most effective in fulfilling their organization's mission, rather than having those funds coercively sent to the federal government to be squandered.

-    -   -

In *The 2020 Initiative* we recommend the establishment of four "pass-through" national charities that would collect charitable contributions for food, housing, education, and healthcare. Citizens would make these contributions, based on which charity they would like to support. Each charity would then have a pool of funds that it would remit to the states. We make this recommendation under the condition that these pass-through entities would be totally free from the political machinations of Washington DC.

These charities would simply collect funds, process the necessary paperwork, and remit the collected funds back to the 50 states, based solely on the data regarding "need" that is collected each year by the IRS on annual income tax returns. Each charity's funds would be distributed to the states based solely on the number of citizens in each state who are requesting financial assistance / welfare. To further help remove the influence of politics on these charities' operations, maybe these charities should be located in America's heartland (like maybe Iowa). Our federal government could save a substantial amount of money by transforming (and essentially eliminating) the Departments of Education, Health & Human Services, Housing & Urban Development, and Agriculture.

-    -   -

In addition to 100% tax credits for donations to these four national pass-through charities, taxpayers should be able to get a 50% tax credit for contributions to their own local community groups, religious organizations, and local social services agencies, to ensure that the money is kept locally and targeted to the group(s) that each taxpayer would like to support. There are already several websites, such as CharityWatch.org, CharityNavigator.org, Give.org, GuideStar.org, and GiveWell.org that are available to assist taxpayers in making their decisions on where their donations would be most effective. These sites provide information on a charity's operations, including Program Expenditures in comparison to their "overhead", the governance and transparency of their operations, and the salaries of top employees of the charity. Information that is included in the organization's annual tax filing (Form 990) is also available to the public on some of these sites, to assist taxpayers in their decision making.

-    -   -

Here is a perverse federal income tax policy - - If you and/or your family don't make enough money, you don't have the same Personal Responsibility as other citizens to file an annual (truthful) income tax return. Does this somehow perversely encourage citizens to operate in the underground economy? (Possibly?? - - Didn't Al Capone get tripped up by this requirement?) Also, does this somehow perversely incentivize people to not make enough income, so they can avoid having the Personal Responsibility to file a tax return with the federal government? Shouldn't we be able to make the process of filing an annual tax return less complicated?

- - -

One of the changes we are recommending in *The 2020 Initiative* is to require every citizen to be accounted for every year via an annual federal income tax return. This recommendation is not being put forward in order to require the poor to pay taxes - - No one should have to pay federal income taxes until they have earned enough income to cover the applicable federal poverty guideline amount. The primary reason for this requirement is to establish a process whereby the government can annually determine whether an individual / family should continue to receive welfare benefits for the upcoming year, and whether that individual / family is making progress on their journey towards self-sufficiency. The Social Security Administration should evolve into an organization that moves away from being a "dispenser of cash benefits" to a consultative organization that can direct people in need towards the appropriate charities and local social services agencies, and assist these individuals / families on their journey out of poverty.

- - -

In addition to establishing eligibility for welfare benefits, there are several other benefits that arise from a requirement that every US citizen be accounted for each year in connection with the annual tax return process. All of the pertinent data that the federal government needs to possess on individual citizens is already included in the Social Security Administration's database (name, address, date of birth, and Social Security number). And the information that is submitted on the tax return identifies all of the individuals that are included within that family unit for that year. If you truly believe in a color blind society and in the concept of Favoritism to None, there isn't any reason for the federal government to gather or maintain any other information on our country's citizens (such as heritage or race).

The annual update of the SSA's database of all US citizens should allow the government to avoid having to perform an expensive census every ten years.

We recommend that the GAO (Government Accountability Office) oversee the reconciliation of the number of citizens per the IRS and the SSA each year. The GAO can also assist the United State Census Bureau in performing a "hard scrub" of the SSA database every ten years, in lieu of performing a separate "once every ten years" census.

The information in the SSA's database would also be the definitive source of data for use by other government agencies. This information should be utilized by the United States Citizenship and Immigration Services to resolve any questions about citizenship or immigration status. We also recommend that the SSA database be updated each year in regards to visas and green cards, along with the reporting of US income earned by non-citizens that is reported to the Internal Revenue Service.

This definitive data on our country's citizens should also be pushed out each year to the 50 states' Board of Elections, to ensure that every state maintains clean voter rolls.

- - -

During the 1930s, the federal government established the Works Progress Administration (WPA) to employ millions of people to carry out public works projects. Our Editorial Board does not advocate the re-creation of a similar agency, but we do suggest that there are a number of "minimal skills level" positions that need to be filled within federal, state, and local governmental units and the Not-for-Profit sector. As we noted above in regards to a transformed Social Security Administration, we suggest that the local SSA office be kept apprised of all job openings within their area in the government sector and in the Not-for-Profit sector. Welfare recipients should be encouraged to pursue these openings as a first step towards re-establishing employment, and which could ultimately lead to a higher level position within such an organization, or ultimately into a better paying job in the private sector.

- - -

Scottish history professor Alexander Tytler (1747-1813) once observed that "A democracy will continue to exist up until the time that voters discover that they can vote themselves generous gifts from the public treasury. From that moment on, the majority always votes for the candidates who promise the most benefits from the public treasury, with the result that every democracy will finally collapse due to loose fiscal policy." Tytler also warned us that the world's greatest civilizations have all progressed through the following sequence: from bondage to spiritual faith, from spiritual faith to great courage, from courage to liberty, from liberty to abundance, from abundance to complacency, from complacency to apathy, from apathy to dependence, and from dependence back into bondage.

\-   \-   \-

There is about $180 billion worth of gold in Ft. Knox. The federal government's deficit for the fiscal year ending on September 30, 2017 is expected to be approximately $600 billion. The total "on book" debt of the federal government as of September 30, 2017 (excluding the present value of Social Security and Medicare "promises") is in excess of $20 trillion.

Contrary to the accounting practices that must be followed by businesses in the private sector, the federal government does not currently record nor report the present value of unfunded pensions and post-retirement obligations that have been promised under Social Security and Medicare. However, these (huge) amounts are disclosed in the Social Security and Medicare Trustees' annual reports. The present value of unfunded Social Security "promises" is $15.4 trillion, and the present value of Medicare "promises" is $33.5 trillion. Even though our country's citizens are finally beginning to become alarmed about the $20 trillion of "on book" debt, they haven't even begun to focus (yet) on the $48.9 trillion of "off book" liabilities that have been promised by our federal government.

Isn't it "funny" that businesses in the private sector are required to account for, and disclose, the present value of these kinds of promises?

\-   \-   \-

Our federal government's growing debt problem represents a complete and unequivocal failure of country's leadership. Congress controls the purse strings. Well, sort of, when you exclude "mandatory" spending. But Congress could control that too, if they had the political will to do so. Our country's Founders warned us about politicians bribing us with our own money (or in the case of deficits and debt, our children's and grandkid's money). They also warned us about human nature, and how easy it would be for our elected officials to create an elite "governing class". Congress' approval rating is at a historic low. And yet over 98% of congressional incumbents who ran for re-election in the last cycle kept their seats in the House and Senate. It is time to change the Constitution, and implement Term Limits for members of the US House of Representatives and the US Senate.

Unfortunately, it appears that Congress will never move forward with an amendment to establish Term Limits for themselves. In 1996, GOP Leadership brought to a vote, in both the House and Senate, a constitutional amendment. It failed to secure the necessary two-thirds vote in the House, where 80 percent of Republicans voted for it and 80 percent of Democrats voted against it. Every Senate Republican voted to allow a vote on term limits, but the Democrats killed it by a filibuster.

Fortunately, our country's Founders provided We-the-People with the means to work around such a Congressional roadblock. Under Article V of the Constitution, all it requires is to have 34 of the 50 states call for a Convention of States. Such a convention would propose amendments to the US Constitution to impose fiscal restraints on the federal government, limit the power and jurisdiction of the federal government, and limit the terms of office for its officials and for members of Congress. We encourage every citizen to visit the website *www.conventionofstates.com* to learn more about the Article V solution, because...... *whenever any form of government becomes destructive to these ends, it is the right of the people to alter or to abolish it, and to institute new government.*

As we have mentioned elsewhere on our website, our Editorial Board does not believe that there is anything fundamentally wrong with the way the US Constitution was written. In fact, it's still a pretty good "social contract" that should not be abolished. However, the liberal/progressive movement has "fundamentally transformed" some of the key principles that were laid out by our country's Founders. The Left has generally ignored many of the warnings that were laid out in the Federalist Papers and in Thomas Paine's pamphlet entitled *Common Sense*. Therefore, our Editorial Board believes that the time has come for We-the-People to (slightly) alter our social contract, by implementing Term Limits, and imposing fiscal restraints on our federal government.

Newsletter No. 1   January 2014

Welcome to our inaugural newsletter.
We hope you had a happy holiday season.

Our Editorial Board is pleased to report the successful launch of our website last month, along with the sign up of our initial Members. We believe that we have a very solid Foundation with our initial Members, who share our concerns about the growth of the federal government, and our country's annual deficit and cumulative debt. Our Foundation's Members are committed to Joining the Conversation, forwarding our website's link (F2PPR.org) to their families, friends and neighbors, and offering up new thoughts and recommendations on how We-the-People can affect the political process, to help solve some of our country's most vexing problems.

As you are probably aware, last month the US House of Representatives and US Senate passed legislation regarding the federal budget for the fiscal year that began last October 1st. You may have read the following encouraging "sound bites" for this accomplishment –

For the first time in what seems like ages, Congress has passed a government spending plan without resorting to last-minute brinkmanship such as midnight negotiations to prevent an imminent government shutdown.

The legislation increases the spending cap to $1.012 trillion for fiscal 2014, and reduces the deficit by about $23 billion over 10 years.

The important fact that is missing from the above snippets is that last month's legislation only dealt with the discretionary portion of federal spending. It should also be noted that the amounts in the legislation exceed the spending caps for fiscal 2014 that had previously been approved by Congress.

Total federal spending for fiscal 2014 in the President's proposed budget (which includes both mandatory and discretionary amounts) is $3.778 trillion. The projected deficit in the President's budget for fiscal 2014 is $744 billion. While this amount is down somewhat from the latest estimate of the deficit for 2013, a $744 billion deficit for 2014 represents an additional $2,300 increase in the amount of debt per citizen – for every man, woman and child in the country.

On our website, we have included a link to the US Debt Clock. On January 1, 2014, the federal government's "on book" debt (i.e., excluding the net present value of future payments for Social Security, Medicare and other promised benefits) was $17.27 trillion, which equates to $54,426 for each US citizen. The main stream media has an obligation to report this cumulative amount per citizen, along with the additional increase that is now incorporated into the federal government's budget for fiscal 2014. Lastly, to put the above "accomplishment" into perspective, $23 billion over 10 years represents an average of $2.3 billion per year, which equates to $7.25 per citizen per year.

Our elected representatives' next big hurdle will be the decisions that need to be made in regards to the country's debt ceiling. The October deal that re-opened the federal government after a 16-day shut down suspended the country's debt limit until February 7th. We will give you an update on this issue in next month's newsletter.

In the meantime, our Editorial Board would like to share with you the following link to a concise overview of our country's annual deficit and debt problems. It is a 13 minute video prepared by David M. Walker, the former Comptroller General of the federal government. If nothing else, please be sure to watch the last two minutes of this video.
(The good news is - - at least we're better than Greece)....

http://www.youtube.com/watch?v=hsUdK70Jtmc&list=SP2ubKCqe8LPUVx qkaV6JZT5a3Pxe2NRgs

We would like to close our inaugural newsletter with our Foundation's motto: If not us, who?   If not now, when?

Keep the faith. We can get this fixed.....

Newsletter No. 2   **February 2014**
The State of the Union

As many of you are aware, President Obama delivered his State of the Union speech on Tuesday night, January 28th. Our Editorial Board was extremely pleased when, six minutes into his speech, the president acknowledged that what *unites the people of this nation, regardless of race, or region, or party, young or old, rich or poor, is the simple, profound belief in opportunity for all; the notion that if you work hard, and take responsibility, you can get ahead in America.* As we all know, this is the basic premise of our Foundation to Promote Personal Responsibility.

However, we were extremely disappointed that the president did not put forward any plan to fix the country's growing debt problem. Instead, the "sound bite" that he included in his speech was -

Our deficits – cut by more than half. However, as we know, that statement simply means that the federal government's debt is not being repaid, but instead continues to grow (more on that later).

Our Editorial Board recognizes that it will take a long time (many years) for our country to repay its debt, and we acknowledge that cutting the deficit is preferable to having the amount of the annual deficit grow each year. However, the federal government is not accomplishing what it needs to do - - cut spending and generate the necessary surpluses to begin repaying the debt. Much of the remainder of the president's speech was devoted to discussing additional programs that the federal government should initiate (without any mention of how those programs would be funded).

In our monthly newsletter, we intend to keep you informed about the amount of the incurred "on-book" debt per US citizen (i.e., the amount of "on-book" debt, which does not even include the present value of the future payments that have been promised for Social Security and Medicare). According to the US Debt clock, this amount of debt per citizen increased from $54,426 as of January 1st to $54,544 as of February 1st.

As many of you are aware, once the federal government was "re-opened" last October, the next key date became February 7th, when the country's debt ceiling needed to be addressed. We are extremely disappointed to report that during the week of February 10th, the US House of Representatives and the US Senate passed legislation to suspend any limitations on the US debt until March 2015. This legislation was signed into law by President Obama on Saturday, February 15th. In effect, our elected officials have written themselves a blank check on your (and, if applicable, your children's) bank account for the next thirteen months.

We would also like to mention that on February 4th the nonpartisan Congressional Budget Office released its annual budget and economic outlook. We are providing the following link to an in-depth analysis prepared by the Committee for a Responsible Federal Budget –

http://crfb.org/sites/default/files/report_analysis_of_cbos_2014_budget_and_economic_outlook.pdf

The main messages are –

- Although the country's deficit levels will decrease this year and next, the annual deficit will begin growing again within two years.

- Almost nothing has been done to finance or slow the growth of "entitlement programs", which are the main drivers of our long-term debt.
- Unless changes are made, both spending and taxes will remain above historical average for the next decade, and will continue to grow over time, and annual deficits in excess of one trillion dollars will return early next decade.
- Interest payments on the country's debt will quadruple in nominal terms between 2013 and 2024.
- By 2020, interest payments on the cumulative US debt will exceed the level of all non-defense discretionary spending.

The Congressional Budget Office's projections are further evidence that the country's annual deficit and cumulative debt problems are far from resolved. The Campaign to Fix the Debt, the Congressional Budget Office, the Committee for a Responsible Federal Budget, and our Foundation all join together, to encourage our elected leaders to work toward reducing the amount of federal expenditures, and ultimately reduce the amount of our country's debt. Please refer to our Conversation Piece on *What the Federal Government Should (and Should Not) Do*, and our recommendations for spending reductions, to restructure the size of the federal government.

In closing, we want to highlight (and applaud) the final comments President Obama made in his State of the Union speech - *Our freedom, our democracy, has never been easy.... But for more than two hundred years, we have... expand(ed) the possibility of individual achievement....so that the words set to paper by our Founders are made real for every citizen. The America we want for our kids – a rising America where honest work is plentiful and communities are strong, where prosperity is widely shared and opportunity for all lets us go as far as our dreams and toil will take us – none of it is easy. But...I know it's within our reach. Believe it.*

We share the president's sentiments. Keep the faith. We can get this fixed.....

Newsletter No. 3   March 2014
If not us, who?   If not now, when?

Last month, we talked about President Obama's State of the Union speech and the lack of any plan to address the country's growing debt problem. We also reported on the legislation that was passed by the US House of Representatives and US Senate to suspend any limitation on the amount of US debt until March 2015.

In this month's newsletter, we would like to address the president's proposal to increase the federal minimum wage from $7.25 per hour to $10.10 per hour. As discussed elsewhere on our website, our Foundation promotes the concept of Personal Responsibility, rather than another government program. In addition, our Editorial Board *hold(s) the following truths to be self-evident* – Poverty sucks – it is estimated that approximately 46 million citizens (roughly 15% of the population) live in poverty

The current poverty level for an individual (as published by the federal government) is $11,490

The current poverty level published by the federal government for a family of four is $23,550

For 2,080 hours of work (no overtime or vacation time) $7.25 per hour is $15,080

For 2,080 hours of work (no overtime or vacation time) $10.10 per hour is $21,008

From a purely monetary perspective, a "minimal wage" job (however defined) sucks

From any perspective, wanting to have a job, but not having a job, really sucks

In a [primarily] free-market, capitalistic economy, prices are affected by supply and demand

In a free-market economy, economic decisions are made after consideration of costs and benefits

The US participates in the global economy, and the level of globalization is increasing each year

Our Editorial Board believes that an individual's personal economic well-being is a Personal Responsibility. But for every belief, there can be an alternative contrarian belief. As we noted on our website, Mitt Romney once made the following observation - *There are... people who are dependent upon government, who believe that they are victims, who believe the government has a responsibility to care for them, who believe that they are entitled to healthcare, to food, to housing, to you-name-it. That's an entitlement. The government should give it to them.*

However, as we noted in that Conversation Piece, our Editorial Board does not believe that the number of people who feel they are a victim totals 47%. But the proponents of the two opposing viewpoints (Personal Responsibility versus a Government Program) have (and hold on to) their own personal beliefs. Our Editorial Board believes that a proposal to increase the minimum wage issue is a very effective "sound bite"- - it speaks to each of us as a caring person and our tendency to want to "do something". However, as we have noted elsewhere, we believe that there are way too many examples of government programs that "sounded good", but then we subsequently find out that all of the implications were not thought through very well, and we find ourselves in a situation where we have "unintended consequences", and the president's proposal is one more example.

Our Editorial Board believes that increasing the minimum wage is counter-productive in solving poverty problems. There are two basic, fundamental (and generally accepted) economic realities (supply and demand, along with "cost versus benefit" decision making) that virtually guarantee that increasing the minimum wage will serve to eliminate a certain number of jobs. It should be noted that different studies project different numbers of jobs lost, but none of the studies show that increasing the minimum wage will serve to increase the number of jobs.

This is how decision making happens in the (real) business world - - faced with a new higher mandated cost, businesses will analyze the economics and the alternatives, and if appropriate, may choose to shift these extra costs into equipment in lieu of minimum wage job(s). The demand for workers will decrease due to higher mandated wage costs, but the supply of available potential employees will remain the same (or probably increase). New higher mandated costs will either be passed on to the market place (which increases inflation) or (if the business is not able to pass on these higher costs in the marketplace) the higher wage costs will negatively impact the business' profitability, and therefore the business' ability to continue to stay in business (and provide jobs).

Minimum wage jobs are merely the first rung on a person's economic ladder. These types of jobs were never intended to be the kind of job that a person should strive for, in order to support a family of four. These jobs are typically filled by high school kids, or by people who are trying to get into the workforce for the first time to establish their skills credentials, or by senior citizens who want to continue to work for personal reasons and who would prefer to get some level of pay rather than perform volunteer work, etc., etc. A minimum wage job has minimal skill requirements - - the primary ones being the ability and the consistency to show up for work each day, take direction from management, be pleasant to work with, and to competently fulfill that job's duties and responsibilities. Unfortunately, developing and maintaining these minimal skills can be a challenge for some individuals, and this is where the public education system and/or social services agencies (and Not-for-Profit organizations) need the public's support, so that these organizations can become more effective in fulfilling their role(s) to help eliminate poverty. This support can include joining your local PTA, running for the local school board, or providing monetary support to these organizations, etc. In order to achieve a higher level of pay, higher paying jobs require higher levels of skills (ie, higher level math and language skills and/or specialized skills). Our Foundation believes that it is the individual's Personal Responsibility to acquire those skills, so that they can find the type of job (or career) that they would like to have, to fulfill their own personal dreams and aspirations. It should be noted that sometimes those dreams and aspirations evolve into a desire to own your own business that would employ your fellow citizens.

The "political sound bite" regarding the minimum wage needs to be re-focused away from the purely "emotional argument" (poverty sucks, so "we the public" are obligated to try and do something) and the conversation needs to be re-directed towards the role of Personal Responsibility, along with society working on finding effective solutions to the issue of poverty in America.

In closing, our Editorial Board would like to mention that we also hold the following truth to be self-evident - - in a free-market, capitalistic economy "income inequality" is merely a fact of life. History has shown that even Communism was unsuccessful in eliminating income inequality (or poverty). Next month we will talk about the president's proposal for the government to solve this "problem".

US Debt Clock - - February 1st - $54,544 per citizen / March 1st - $54,729

Newsletter No. 4   April 2014

As we noted last month, President Obama, in his State of the Union speech, discussed the need to find a solution to the problem of "income inequality". One of his proposals is to raise the minimum wage to $10.10 per hour. However, based on the Congressional Budget Office's analysis of his proposal, it is a much better "sound bite" than an effective policy. Increasing the minimum wage would serve to decrease the country's poverty rate by less than half a percent, and the $31 billion "extra tax" on businesses *would not go to only low-income families, because many low-wage workers are not members of low-income families. Just 19% of the $31 billion would accrue to families with earnings below the poverty threshold, whereas 29% would accrue to families earning more than three times the poverty threshold.* [The remaining 52% of the $31 billion would also go to families above the government's poverty threshold]. Our Editorial Board believes that there are more effective ways to address poverty in America.

Some of our readers may be aware that a documentary was released last fall, which was entitled *Inequality for All*. It features the viewpoints of Robert Reich, who was Secretary of Labor during President Clinton's first term. Our Editorial Board agrees with a number of Mr. Reich's observations, but we also take exception to some of his conclusions. Early in the documentary, Mr. Reich acknowledges that within the US economy "some inequality is inevitable" - - it is the essence of capitalism. Capitalism fosters innovation, creativity and enterprise, and it rewards taking Personal Responsibility for your own economic well-being. We agree with Mr. Reich's observation that the US economy is not a purely capitalistic / purely "free market" system. We agree that one of the roles of government is to set the rules and regulations by which the market functions, and therefore (rightly or wrongly) the government's rules help determine who benefits and who is hurt by those policies and programs.

We also agree with Mr. Reich's observation (and the underlying data) that the inflation-adjusted income of the average US worker began to flatten out during the 1970s, primarily due to the effects of globalization and new technologies. Robotics, self-scanning check-out lines, and other changes in the workplace have eliminated certain jobs. Some people curse the effects of progress and change; our Editorial Board embraces creativity, innovation, progress and change. However, this raises an interesting question - Does this mean that workers today (more so than at any other point in time) need to continue learning after they finish their formal education? Absolutely.

Here are some of Mr. Reich's other observations about income inequality - - The disparity in annual income/wealth between "the Top 1%" and the average/median for the country as a whole has steadily increased over the past 30-40 years, and peaked in 2007 - - we agree with the data. Our country's overall economy has grown tremendously during the past 30-40 years. Therefore "income inequality" is primarily a mathematical result - - when the economy has grown tremendously, and the average/median income has grown only slightly, there is an increase in the mathematical disparity.

One of Mr. Reich's hypotheses is that this concentration of wealth leads to "speculative investments" (ie, in housing) which contribute to the formation of various "asset bubbles" which inevitably burst, and which led to the great recession of 2008-2009. However, he does not acknowledge that the government's own loosening of the rules relating to the requirements/qualifications to obtain a mortgage also significantly contributed to this asset bubble. In addition, as Mr. Reich correctly points out, many people did not diligently pay down their mortgage balance (to ensure that they would never lose their home) but instead used their home as an ATM. (Plus, the government allows mortgage interest to be a deductible expense for tax purposes). It is generally accepted that sub-prime mortgages were one of the major triggers that led to the great recession. As we noted above, we agree that the government does have an important role to play in establishing rules and regulations to protect the public (in this case, from ourselves).

We also agree with one of Mr. Reich's main warnings about income inequality - - the increasing concentration of wealth does create a danger to democracy. With money, comes the possibility to control government. The *Inequality for All* documentary was fairly even-handed in that it identified several wealthy individuals who have made significant contributions to either liberal causes or conservative causes (according to each contributor's tendency). Unfortunately, the Supreme Court has ruled that campaign contributions by corporations and wealthy individuals, in effect, cannot be limited, as this represents a restriction on the freedom of speech. There is a reason for the expression "Money talks", and money does buy influence. As an alternative, our Foundation supports the concept of Term Limits. We need to find different ways (i.e., CHANGE THE RULES) to reduce the possibility that our elected officials become entrenched, and become beholden to special interests, rather than to the interests of the country as a whole. We believe that if our elected officials are elected for a set (limited) period of time, they will have a greater tendency to serve the public good, rather than focus on worrying about their next re-election.

So, who is the "Top 1%"? The income level for the Top 1% is an annual income over $380,000. The Top 1% includes some professional people (doctors, lawyers), some entrepreneurs/business owners/venture capitalists/risk takers, some corporate CEOs, certain elected officials at both the national and state levels, professional athletes, entertainers, etc.

One last set of data to be considered (this is IRS tax data for 2011) - - The Top 1% of US taxpayers paid a greater share of all federal income taxes in 2011 (35.1%) than the entire bottom 90% (31.7%). The 1,366,000 taxpayers in the Top 1% (who earned approximately 20% of the country's total personal income) paid over 35% of the total income taxes paid to the federal government, so it's not like the Top 1% isn't already covering a relatively higher share of the total tax load. We agree that they should - - Please re-visit our website and see our Conversation Pieces on Tax Rationalization, Tax Reform, and Tax Simplification issues. Just to clarify... There were approximately 136.6 million personal income tax returns filed for 2011. This is substantially less than the US population of 317 million US citizens, primarily due to "Married Filing Jointly" tax returns (with or without dependent children), along with a number of citizens who do not file an income tax return.

Having said all that.... We also agree with the comments that were made by Warren Buffet and Nick Hanauer in the documentary - - The US tax code is screwed up - - they only paid an effective tax rate of 17.7% / 11% on their incomes, which were in excess of $10 million. As Mr. Reich points out, it is the federal government that sets the rules. At the end of the day, this is what the political process is all about. This is why We-the-People need to Join the Conversation and get more involved in the process, to debate (and find better solutions to) the issues that are being discussed.

- - - - -

Our Editorial Board also recently reviewed a commentary that was published a few months ago by one of our favorite columnists, Cal Thomas - - **Income Inequality is Part of the Entitlement Philosophy.** The primary points that Mr. Thomas makes in his commentary are that certain political leaders *want us to accept a false premise: that if I earn more money than you, I "owe" you some of my money to make things "fair"..... "Income inequality" is a part of the greed-envy-entitlement philosophy promoted by liberals who want to addict more people to government..... There was a time when Americans would have been ashamed to take, much less ask for, anything from their fellow citizens.... Envy, greed and entitlements are not the things that built America..... The concern should not be how much others make, but how much you can make if you apply yourself and adopt the values embraced by successful people.* Thank you, Cal - we couldn't have said it any better.

- - - - -

On March 4, President Obama submitted his budget for fiscal 2015. We will address the president's proposed budget in next month's newsletter. The unfortunate news is that, for each of the next ten years projected in the president's budget, there is not a single year that shows anything other than a continuation of annual deficits. Evidently, our country's game plan is to let the amount of debt per citizen continue to grow each year. Our Editorial Board believes that (contrary to the president's plan) we CAN get this fixed.

OK, one more set of data - - Even if the federal government were to "appropriate" (i.e., steal) the entire net worth (the accumulated wealth) of the country's Top 100 billionaires (i.e., Bill Gates, Warren Buffet, George Soros, Oprah Winfrey, Mark Zuckerberg, etc.) the government would be able to pay-off only a fraction (less than 7.5%) of the $17.5 trillion "on book" US debt (which excludes the future negative cash flows for Social Security and Medicare benefits that have also been promised). Even the very richest people in the country cannot begin to pay off our country's debt, so who is going to pay it off? This intergenerational debt obligation (which is being pushed onto our children and grandchildren by our federal government) is immoral. We MUST get this fixed.

US Debt Clock (the "on book" US debt) - - March 1st - $54,729 per citizen / April 1st - $55,228

Newsletter No. 5   May 2014

As we noted last month, President Obama has submitted his proposed budget for fiscal 2015. The link to the president's proposed budget is

http://www.gpo.gov/fdsys/pkg/BUDGET-2015-BUD/pdf/BUDGET-2015-BUD.pdf

The budget document includes projections for the next ten years, all of which show a continuation of annual deficits. The estimated deficit for the current fiscal year ending on September 30, 2014 is $649 billion and the deficit anticipated for fiscal 2015 is $564 billion. These deficits represent an additional amount of debt per citizen (for every man, woman, retiree and child) of $2,000 for fiscal 2014 and $1,800 for next year, which get added on top of the current amount of $55,000 per citizen. David Walker, the former Comptroller General of the federal government (see our January newsletter) calls this an "unsustainable path". We agree.

The following is an overview of the federal government's budget, along with the average compound growth rates that take us 10 years into the future, from 2014 to 2024 (in billions) –

	2014	2024	Ave CGR
Receipts	$3,002	$5,478	6.2%
Outlays	3,651	5,912	4.9%
Deficit	$(649)	$(434)	

On our website, we have noted the ever-expanding growth of the federal government in comparison to the economy as a whole. The president's budget is built to continue this ever-expanding role. While we "applaud" the reduction in the amount of the deficit, we are dismayed that there continues to be a deficit each year. And we question why the government's receipts need to increase faster than the growth of the overall economy. The federal government's Receipts as a percent of GDP increase from 17.3% in 2014 to 19.9% in 2024.

So what is driving this shift, and what is driving the federal government's role in our economy to even higher levels in the future? Two of the major components of the amounts shown above are Social Security and Medicare/Medicaid –

Social Security -

	2014	2024	Ave CGR
Receipts	$ 732	$1,191	5.0%
Outlays	852	1,499	5.8%
Deficit	$(120)	$(308)	

Medicare / Medicaid -

	2014	2024	Ave CGR
Receipts	$ 219	$ 368	5.3%
Outlays	821	1,503	6.2%
Deficit	$(602)	$(1,135)	

A wise journalist once wrote – You can either have Big Government or you can have Lower Taxes, but you can't have both. Unfortunately, our elected officials in Washington continue to try to circumvent this basic fact. To their credit, our elected officials have been somewhat successful in accomplishing this feat, however, they have accomplished this by "borrowing" these funds from future generations (some of who cannot yet vote, and some who have not even been born yet).

US Debt Clock - - April 1st - $55,228 per citizen / May 1st - $55,069
Please do not be overly encouraged by the decrease noted above. This effect typically happens during early April. Tax refunds are sent out over the course of the tax filing season, however, taxpayers who owe money typically don't pay their remaining balance due until shortly before the tax filing deadline. We will give you another update on the amount of debt per citizen in next month's newsletter.

Newsletter No. 6   June 2014

So, the question seems to be - - Does the annual deficit and the cumulative US debt really matter? It is apparent that many of our elected officials believe that the answer to this question is "No". As we mentioned last month, President Obama has submitted his proposed budget, which shows a continuation of annual deficits for at least the next ten years. And as you recall, last October the members of the US Senate and the US House of Representatives decided to "write themselves a blank check" and suspend the country's debt ceiling until after the 2014 elections. (More on Term Limits in next month's newsletter).

One of the reasons why our elected officials can avoid addressing the growing debt problem is that most US citizens are not aware that our federal government has run up a + $17 trillion cumulative debt (an amount in excess of $55,000 per citizen). But the US economy continues to recover from the Great Recession, so the cumulative federal government debt must not be an issue - - right??

One of the reasons why the growing debt problem has not yet affected the US economy is because the US dollar is (currently) the "world's reserve currency" - - the US dollar is widely held around the world, and most international transactions are conducted and settled using the US dollar. Because of the dollar's status as the world's reserve currency, this has allowed the federal government to simply print more dollars, and over the past several years, the Federal Reserve has purchased this new money (through "Quantitative Easing") which has kept interest rates artificially low. The thinking seems to be that as long as inflation and interest rates can be successfully manipulated downward, there will never be a day of reckoning for the growing debt problem. Beside, the US dollar is backed by "the full faith and credit of the federal government".

But what happens if the rest of the world begins to lose faith in the creditworthiness of the US dollar? The British pound used to be the world's reserve currency, but once the British pound lost that distinction, there were significant, severe effects on the British economy, which took many painful years to fix. History is full of examples where a government's mis-handling of its economy and its currency has had dire consequences - - Germany in the 1920s, the United Kingdom in the 1970s, Argentina in the 1980s, Argentina from 1999 to 2002, Iceland in 2008, Greece in 2009 - - the list goes on and on.

Although the US economy / US dollar appropriately earned its position as being the world's reserve currency, there is no guarantee that this will continue in the future. In fact, the process has already begun - - the Euro has replaced the US dollar for cross border transactions within Europe, and many other international transactions are now being conducted and settled using currencies other than the US dollar. In addition, the major credit rating agencies downgraded the US in 2011, primarily because the federal government increased the debt ceiling (and the cumulative US debt has increased substantially since then).

So…. How long can the Federal Reserve and the federal government print money and manipulate interest rates downward? Our Editorial Board members are not economists, and we do not possess a crystal ball that provides the answer to that question. However, we bring a business perspective to our analysis of the government's fiscal policies, and we agree with David Walker (the former Comptroller General of the federal government) that the trajectory of the cumulative US debt is on an unsustainable path. As a country, We-the-People cannot borrow and spend ourselves into prosperity. Once interest rates begin to rise again, for every 1% increase in interest rates, the federal government's annual interest cost will go up by $170 billion, and this amount would get layered on top of the existing annual deficit, which is budgeted to be another $564 billion for fiscal 2015. The question is not "if" the growing US debt is a problem - - the questions are "when will it become a severe problem" and "how severe"?

US Debt Clock - - May 1st - $55,069 per citizen / June 1st - $55,072 (a relatively "good" month)

Newsletter No. 7   July 2014

As we have noted on our Foundation's website, our Editorial Board believes that our country's Founders did an excellent job in preparing the "social contract" between the citizens and their government (i.e., the US Constitution). We also noted that in several of the Federalist Papers that were written prior to the ratification of the Constitution, our country's Founders recognized the need *to guard as effectually as possible against a perversion of power to the public detriment…. The means relied on… for preventing their* [elected officials] *degeneracy are numerous and various – the most effectual one is such a limitation on the term of appointments as will maintain a proper responsibility to the people.*

In addition to our Foundation, there are several other organizations that also support the concept of Term Limits. Please visit the US Term Limits (USTL) site at www.termlimits.org. USTL's purpose is to support *a government of the people, by the people, and for the people, not a tyrannical ruling class who care more about deals to benefit themselves, rather than their constituents.* We encourage you to sign the USTL Congressional Term Limits petition, and support the passage of the Term Limits Amendment put forward by US Senator Jim DeMint.

It should be noted that the counter-argument to Term Limits is that there already exists a means to limit an elected official's time in office - - it's called the election cycle. While there is some merit to this line of thinking, our

Editorial Board rejects that argument, because we question why any group of citizens would ever want to vote out of office an elected official that their efforts helped put into that office. As we all learned in school, George Washington was adamantly opposed to the idea of an "imperial presidency" and vowed to serve at most only two terms. [His presidency was nearly 200 years prior to the ratification of the 22nd Amendment].

Although Term Limits will never be the sole solution to our country's political problems, our Editorial Board believes that Term Limits will serve to combat many of the ills that have crept into our country's political process - - Pork, Pork Barrel Politics, Bringing Home the Bacon, Influence Peddling, Lobbyists, Pandering, Conflicts of Interest, Patronage, Nepotism, Cronyism, Graft, Corruption, etc. We believe that Term Limits are appropriate for all Executive and Legislative positions at both the federal and state level. For legislative positions especially, it is highly unlikely that the constituents of a district would ever vote out an incumbent, as long as that person is effective in Bringing Home the Bacon.

We-the-People need to take back control of our governmental units from career politicians, whose power and influence only grows larger, the longer they are in office. We need to return to the original intent of the country's Founders – a government of the people, by the people (the citizenry) rather than career politicians. Our Editorial Board agrees with the following well-known quote, which is attributed to Lord Acton (a British historian) - *Power corrupts, and absolute power corrupts absolutely*.

The primary benefit of Term Limits is that limiting the time someone is in office should serve to shift the focus of our elected officials away from the "expedient" and towards the greater good for the country as a whole. Our elected officials should not be focused on their next re-election and doling out money to their constituents. Term Limits would allow our elected officials the freedom to pursue policies that might be unpopular with their constituents, but which they know are vitally important to the greater good of the individuals who comprise our nation (such as eliminating deficit spending and then reducing the cumulative US debt).

US Debt Clock - - June 1st - $55,072 per citizen / July 1st - $55,149

Newsletter No. 8   August 2014

This past month the trustees of the Social Security and Medicare "trust funds" released their annual report on the current and projected status of these federal government programs. The trustees' Summary Annual Reports can be found at www.ssa.gov/OACT/TRSUM/index.html

In this month's newsletter, we will focus on Social Security. (Medicare is next month). On our Foundation's website (in the Conversation Piece about Social Security) we discuss the fact that this federal government program is not a Ponzi scheme, but it is not the same as a funded pension plan. Instead, it should be viewed as being an "intergenerational social contract". Unfortunately, many citizens have been misled by the terminology used by our public officials, when they read about Social Security's "trust fund assets". They incorrectly believe that their payroll tax withholdings (along with their employer's contributions) have been set aside in a separate investment pool that will be used to pay future benefits (to which they are "entitled") once they retire. The *inconvenient truth* about Social Security is that the only "assets" owned by the trust are intergovernmental loans receivable. The payroll taxes paid into Social Security have already been paid out for past benefits, or have been "loaned" (spent) for other federal government purposes.

To make matters worse, the annual expenditures for Social Security now exceed the program's inflows, and this adds to the cumulative US debt. In addition, based on President Obama's 2015 budget and the projections through 2024, the annual shortfall grows and compounds each year.

So.... How did this "well intentioned" government program, which was established during the height of the Great Depression, evolve into its current state? There are two key issues - - one "actuarial" problem and one "demographics" problem. The actuarial problem is that people are living longer lives, compared to when Social Security was established in 1935. This "actuarial problem" is not unique to Social Security - it has the same, significant effect on any type of retirement/pension plan. If Social Security were to be accounted for in a manner similar to what is required for corporations' pension plans, the estimated present value of the unfunded future benefits that have been promised is approximately $11.1 trillion. This liability for this "pay as you go" program is over and above the "on book" US debt of $17.6 trillion, which already equates to $55,273 per citizen. (And keep in mind that this amount is for Social Security benefits only - - it excludes the "off book" liability for Medicare, which is a much bigger number - - but that is the topic for next month's newsletter).

The demographics problem is that the relative number of retirees continues to grow as the Baby Boomers move into their retirement years. Once the country got past the Great Depression and World War II, the number of workers for each retiree in 1950 was 16 workers per retiree. In 2014, that ratio is now down to approximately 3, and by 2030 will be down to approximately 2.

Here are some key passages from the trustees' annual report –

For the past several years, the annual Trustees Reports have warned lawmakers and the public of the financing shortfalls facing the Social Security and Medicare programs, emphasizing that continued delay in legislating corrective measures is likely to make the challenge ever more difficult to resolve.....

While Social Security has not been the object of significant financing reforms since 1983, its need for additional measures has been recognized for over two decades. Now, in the middle of the second decade of the 21st century, the adverse consequences of delaying necessary corrections in both programs are beginning to be realized.

Lawmakers should address the financial challenges facing Social Security as soon as possible. Taking action sooner rather than later will leave more options and more time available to phase in changes so that the public has more time to prepare.

It is interesting to note that the "average Joes" and the "average Jills" who understand these issues (and the associated math) are justifiably concerned about the **status of these programs and the country's finances.** Unfortunately (as we noted in last month's newsletter) our Editorial Board believes that because many of our elected officials are more concerned about their own re-election issues, it is easier for them to kick this can down the road to future generations (some of whom cannot even vote yet) rather than **pursue the implementation of policies that they know are vitally important to the country's future.**

US Debt Clock (the "on book" debt) - - July 1st - $55,149 per citizen / August 1st - $55,273

Newsletter No. 9   September 2014

As we discuss on our website in the conversation piece on *Universal Health Care*, Medicare (like Social Security) should be viewed as being an "intergenerational social contract" - - it is not a conventional health insurance program, because the "premiums" paid by senior citizens for their coverage are not a market-based premium. In fact, the primary reason Medicare was established in 1965 is that many senior citizens were no longer able to acquire a health insurance policy at any cost. However, nothing is free, so this cost must be borne by somebody (more on that later).

Similar to Social Security, Medicare's "trust fund assets" (i.e., employees' Medicare payroll tax withholdings, along with their employers' contributions) have already been paid out for past benefits, or have been "loaned" (spent) for other federal government purposes.

Medicare and Medicaid were signed into law on July 30, 1965 by President Lyndon B. Johnson, as part of LBJ's "Great Society" domestic social programs. Medicaid is a welfare program, as there are no cash inflows into the Treasury for Medicaid, other than general tax receipts.

Information on the annual cost of the federal government's healthcare programs can be found in President Obama's proposed budget for fiscal 2015 (the link is in our May newsletter). For the current fiscal year ending this month of September, it is projected that the difference between the cash outflows for Medicare and Medicaid ($513 billion + $308 billion = $821 billion) will exceed the $219 billion collected via Medicare payroll taxes, for a difference (deficit) of $602 billion. Medicare/Medicaid account for nearly all of the $628 billion deficit projected for fiscal 2014.

Unless changes are made to Medicare/Medicaid, this annual deficit amount will grow over the next ten years to $1.135 trillion by 2024 - - the outflow of $947 billion in 2024 for Medicare, plus $556 billion for Medicaid equals $1.5 trillion, versus the projected Medicare payroll tax receipts of $368 billion.

Similar to the Social Security Trustees' report, the Medicare report also includes an estimate of the present value of the "off book" debt amount for Medicare (which is for Medicare only, excluding Medicaid). Please keep in mind that the current cumulative "on-book" US debt amount for our past deficit spending is $17.6 trillion. As we reported in last month's newsletter, the present value of the "off book" debt for the Social Security benefits that have been promised is $11.1 trillion. The "off book" debt for the present value of Medicare benefits that have been promised is $28.5 trillion.

It is safe to say that unless our elected officials begin to make fundamental changes to our country's finances to eliminate deficit spending, this debt (and more) will fall to our children and grandchildren. Our elected officials need to change their focus towards fiscal responsibility, rather than their own personal re-election concerns. Our federal government's first step needs to be the elimination of deficit spending, and once that is accomplished, we then need to begin re-paying the "on book" debt.

US Debt Clock (the "on book" debt) - - August 1st - $55,273 per citizen / September 1st - $55,528

As we have noted on our website, our Foundation supports the efforts of the Campaign to Fix the Debt. We have provided a link on our Home Page to the Campaign's website, and we encourage all citizens to digitally sign the Petition to Fix the Debt. The Campaign has recently published a two-page summary about the Debt Threat, along with another paper that lists some of the Common Myths about the US Debt. There are several reasons why it has become critically important that our elected officials begin to fix this growing problem.

Ever-growing levels of debt threaten citizens' and families' economic well-being in a number of ways -

Lower Wages and Fewer Job Opportunities – As the government continues to issue more and more debt, this debt "crowds out" productive investments in people, machinery, technology and new ventures.

Growing national debt can drive up interest rates throughout the economy, leading to higher interest payments on mortgages, car loans, student loans, and credit card debt.

Interest will represent the fastest growing part of the federal budget. The nonpartisan Congressional Budget Office projects that interest costs will nearly quadruple from about $220 billion in 2013 to almost $880 billion in 2024. As more of our budget goes to financing today's spending and yesterday's promises, spending targeted toward the next generation will continue to dwindle.

A Threatened Social Safety Net – By 2033, the combined Social Security trust funds are expected to run out of money, at which point all beneficiaries will receive an immediate cut in benefits.

An Increased Likelihood of a Fiscal Crisis – Failure to get the national debt under control could precipitate a crisis... International examples suggest there could be large investment losses, tanking markets, sharply rising interest rates, mass unemployment, rapid inflation, and/or devastating austerity, causing sharp drops in public investment.

Some of the common myths about the growing debt problem include –

The amount of the annual deficit is falling, and therefore, debt is no longer a concern.

There is no harm in waiting to solve our debt problems.

As our country's citizens prepare to head to the polls next month, we encourage you to download these publications from the Campaign's website and share them with your family and friends –

The Debt Threat
www.fixthedebt.org/uploads/files/national%20debt%20and%20you%20final.pdf

Common Myths About the Debt
www.fixthedebt.org/uploads/files/Debt%20myths%20and%20facts%20final.pdf

And we encourage you to support those candidates who are campaigning to solve our country's growing debt problem, who are more concerned about the country's future (rather than their own future re-election chances), and who are committed to Fix the Debt, rather than push this growing problem onto future generations.

US Debt Clock - - September 1st - $55,528 per citizen / October 1st - $55,812

Newsletter No. 11   November 2014

Election Day is Tuesday, November 4th. Our Editorial Board encourages you to support those candidates who are running for office to solve our country's growing debt problem. Thomas Jefferson once wrote "If we can but prevent the government from wasting the labours of the people, under the pretence of taking care of them, they must become happy." In the upcoming election, we have an opportunity to choose whether we want to stay on the current path of larger, ever-expanding government, or if we want to heed the advice of one of our country's Founders.

Unfortunately, this past month (which was the first month of our federal government's new fiscal year) our country passed a new threshold. The cumulative US debt now stands in excess of $17.8 trillion, which equates to an amount in excess of $56,000 for every man, woman, child and retiree.

Please give your support to those candidates who are more concerned about our country's future (rather than their own future re-election chances), and who are committed to Fix the Debt, rather than push this growing problem onto future generations.

US Debt Clock - - October 1st - $55,812 per citizen / November 1st - $56,065

Newsletter No. 12   December 2014

OK, so the November elections are over – Now what? The newly elected Senators and members of the House of Representatives take office on January 3, 2015. But before then, the existing "Continuing Resolution" that funds the federal government expires on December 11th. Therefore, sometime during the next few weeks Congress must pass an appropriations bill to keep the federal government operating. A Continuing Resolution doesn't make any changes to the country's spending levels, but merely continues the pre-existing appropriations at the same level as the previous fiscal year. As we noted in our May newsletter, the president's proposed budget for the current fiscal year anticipates an additional deficit of $564 billion, which will further add to the cumulative US debt.

The next key date in 2015 is March 16th, when the country's debt ceiling is re-instated. As we noted last February, the US Senate and House of Representatives "kicked the can down the road" to the new Congress and suspended any limitations on the US debt until March 2015. In effect, they wrote themselves a blank check that has allowed the federal government to continue borrowing money at the expense of future generations. It is our Editorial Board's hope that the new Congress will begin to make the difficult decisions that need to be made, to begin curtailing the size and spending of the federal government and begin repaying the cumulative US debt.

US Debt Clock - - November 1st - $56,065 per citizen / December 1st - $56,266

Newsletter No. 13   January 2015

As we anticipated in last month's newsletter, the US House of Representatives and US Senate recently passed "Continuing Resolution" legislation that funds most of the departments of the federal government through the end of the government's fiscal year on September 30, 2015. While this legislation helped to prevent another government shutdown, the country is virtually guaranteed to incur another deficit this year.

In President Obama's 2015 budget, payroll tax receipts for Social Security are expected to be $756 billion, and spending will be $896 billion, for a deficit of $140 billion. Medicare payroll tax receipts are expected to be $231 billion, and the outflows for Medicare/Medicaid are budgeted to be $860 billion.

We are also sorry to report that the country passed another new milestone this past month - - the cumulative US debt has now risen above $18 trillion.

Thomas Jefferson once wrote - *I wish it were possible to obtain a single amendment to our constitution; I would be willing to depend on that alone for the reduction of the administration of our government to the genuine principles of its constitution; I mean an additional article taking from the federal government the power of borrowing.*

There is another quote that is often attributed to either Alexis de Tocqueville (1805-1859, a French historian most famous for his work *Democracy in America*) or to Alexander Fraser Tytler (1747-1813, a Scottish history professor at the University of Edinburgh) – *A democracy will continue to exist up until the time that voters discover that they can vote themselves generous gifts from the public treasury.* Another variant of this quote is - *The American Republic will endure until politicians realize that they can bribe the people with their own money.*

Margaret Thatcher (the Prime Minister of the United Kingdom from 1979-1990) gave us her own perspective on the issue – *The trouble with Socialism is that eventually you run out of other people's money.*

The link between all three of these quotes is that there has been a collective failure of our country's elected officials, who have chosen to ignore the advice of one of our country's Founders. Instead, they have pushed a huge financial burden onto future generations.

As we noted in our inaugural newsletter a year ago, David Walker, the former Comptroller General of the federal government, put it this way – *This is not just a financial issue. This is not just an economic issue. This is an ethical and moral issue… We are mortgaging the future of our kids and grandkids at record rates…. and it must stop.*

The next key date occurs in March, when the country's debt ceiling needs to be addressed by our elected "leaders". We will keep you posted….

US Debt Clock - - December 1st - $56,266 per citizen / January 1st - $56,356

Newsletter No. 14   February 2015

Our Editorial Board recently ran across an interesting article. For the past several months, consumer debt has been increasing, as American households have become somewhat more confident about the state of the economy. The consumer debt amount that was reported in the article excludes real estate loans, which is probably appropriate, because that type of debt is backed by the associated asset being financed. Consumer debt includes credit card debt, auto loans, student loans, etc, and represents the personal decisions made by American families. This amount has recently risen to a "record level" of $3.3 trillion. Now... Contrast that "record" amount with the $18 trillion that has been borrowed on our collective behalf by our elected officials.

So, how did we get to this $18 trillion record amount? As we noted last month, and as shown in the table below, the growth in the US debt represents a collective failure of both the legislative branch and the executive branch, and by the politicians in both political parties –

Jimmy Carter (1976-1980) $.6T to $.9T – An increase of $.3 trillion

Ronald Reagan (1980-1988) $.9T to $2.6T – An increase of $1.7 trillion

George H.W. Bush (1988-1992) $2.6T to $4.1T – An increase of $1.5 trillion

Bill Clinton (1992-2000) $4.1T to $5.7T – An increase of $1.6 trillion

George W. Bush (2000-2008) $5.7T to $10.0T – An increase of $4.3 trillion

Barack Obama (2008-2015 so far) $10.0T to $18.0T – An increase of $8.0 trillion (so far)

As we have noted in previous newsletters, the primary driver of the annual deficit and our growing debt problem continues to be the country's "entitlement" programs. Starting with FDR's Social Security initiative during the 1930s, the executive branch has played a significant role in transforming the country into what has been termed an "Entitlement State". Additional entitlement programs were established during the 1960s by LBJ's Great Society initiative and the War on Poverty, which brought us Medicare / Medicaid and a number of new welfare programs. The Entitlement State has grown even larger in recent years with the Affordable Care Act (Obamacare), and during the president's most recent State of the Union speech, he proposed that we should establish even more entitlement programs, such as "free" college education.

It should be noted that the US House of Representatives and US Senate are also partly to blame, because our elected representatives are responsible for approving and funding these programs. Our country's financial future has been put at risk by politicians who want to continue to provide generous gifts from the public treasury.

Our Foundation's objective is to promote Personal Responsibility (rather than a constantly expanding set of costly government programs). Our primary agenda item is to re-establish fiscal responsibility by the federal government. We seek to (significantly) reduce the size of the Entitlement State, and re-establish a Self-Reliant Society. Because career politicians have found out that they can stay in office by pandering to special interest groups, and by bribing the citizenry with their own money (and with future generations' money), our Editorial Board believes that one of the best ways to re-establish fiscal responsibility is to implement Term Limits for members of the US House of Representatives and US Senate.

US Debt Clock - - January 1st - $56,356 per citizen / February 1st - $56,533

Newsletter No. 15   March 2015

Last year, the US House of Representatives and US Senate approved legislation to suspend any limitation on the US debt until March 15, 2015. In effect, they wrote themselves a blank check to continue to borrow and spend funds over and above the amount that the government collects in taxes. Our Editorial Board is not very optimistic that any meaningful long-term fix to the country's growing debt problem will be implemented within the next few weeks (but maybe we will be pleasantly surprised for a change).

Last month, we talked about the growth of the Entitlement State and the need to re-establish a Self-Reliant Society. These terms come from a book by Don Watkins, who is an author, columnist and professional speaker. The title of his book is *RooseveltCare*, and the subtitle is *How Social Security is Sabotaging the Land of Self-Reliance*. Mr. Watkins makes a compelling case for eliminating all entitlement programs, starting with Social Security. However, he acknowledges that accomplishing this goal is probably not politically possible, because according to a 2011 national poll, eight out of ten Americans responded that "Social Security has been good for the country". However, keep in mind that this result is primarily due to the fact that politicians have bribed us - - not with our own money, but with the money of future generations.

RooseveltCare does not include any graphs or complicated accounting concepts. It merely tells the story of the role that Social Security and other entitlement programs have played in eroding the eagerness, energy, and optimism that once defined our country. Mr. Watkins makes the case that the Entitlement State is robbing his daughter's generation of many of her hopes and dreams. One of his most pointed assertions is "I am not my grandfather's keeper". Flipping this around, our Editorial Board believes that more than eight out of ten people would be appalled by the thought of stealing money from our children and grandkids. But in effect, this is exactly what is happening. There is no money in the Social Security Trust Fund (or in the Medicare Trust Fund). The only "assets" in the Trusts are "intergenerational wealth transfer arrangements" (i.e., US debt). Every dollar that is spent today to provide these benefits comes directly from current employees' paychecks. Each year, the shortfall between these cash outflows and the payroll taxes collected by the government is simply added to the country's growing debt problem. And the amounts are projected to worsen each year because the number of active employees supporting the Baby Boom generation is now down to less than three workers for each retiree.

We will provide excerpts from Mr. Watkins' book in next month's newsletter. In the meantime, please note that *RooseveltCare* is available in PDF format over the internet. Mr. Watkins is providing this book for "free" (truly) because he feels that the current Entitlement State is unsustainable, and it is time for the country - its citizens and politicians - to finally address the reality that Social Security is a financial black hole, and begin to make the necessary changes.

US Debt Clock - - February 1st - $56,533 per citizen / March 1st - $56,615

Newsletter No. 16   April 2015

As we noted last month, in February 2014 the US House of Representatives and US Senate passed legislation to suspend the country's debt ceiling until

March 15, 2015. Unfortunately, our elected officials chose to not deal with this new deadline. Treasury Secretary Jacob Lew wrote a letter to Congress, asking for an increase to the country's debt ceiling, however, because the country's legislators have not acted to raise the limit, the Treasury Department is implementing "extraordinary measures" to keep the federal government from defaulting on its debt. Some of these measures include putting a stop to contributions into certain federal employees' pension funds, drawing down on other funds, and imposing moratoriums on payments to state and local governments. It is anticipated that these measures will enable the federal government to push the problem off until September or October. Our Editorial Board has been disappointed (yet again) by our elected officials. President Obama's fiscal 2016 budget proposal shows continued (growing) annual deficits out through the year 2025. There does not appear to be any serious discussions about fixing the country's growing debt problem.

Last month, we began a discussion of Don Watkins' book entitled *RooseveltCare (How Social Security is Sabotaging the Land of Self-Reliance)*. In this month's newsletter, we share some excerpts about the creation of Social Security and the beginnings of the Entitlement State - -

It is time to put the myths about Social Security to rest, and replace them with the truth: Social Security is an un-American program.

America was much freer before the Entitlement State. Americans took the Declaration of Independence seriously. The government played the important role of protecting us from criminals and foreign threats, but otherwise left us pretty much alone.

Government welfare "is an un-American thing" said the wife of an unemployed worker during the Great Depression. "It is a dole. No real person with a sense of responsibility wants welfare". ....being on the dole is bad for the recipient, economically and spiritually.

One of our first "Progressive" presidents, Woodrow Wilson, was open in his contempt for America's founding principles - - "It was (Thomas) Jefferson who said that the best government is that which does as little governing as possible... but that time is passed."

Subsequently, FDR got his way with the passage of the Social Security Act of 1935. The 1935 act was funded by a 2 percent tax on wages up to a $3,000 cap. A pamphlet the government created to promote Social Security assured the public, "That *is the most you will ever pay." It was a particularly egregious lie in a campaign built on lies.*

The proponents of welfare benefit rights needed to change people's longstanding view that going on the dole was shameful. "Everybody is entitled." They wanted to end the stigma of dependency. The goal was to "make dependency legitimate."

It's no mystery why we've seen this disintegration of Personal Responsibility. Responsibility flourishes in a society that preaches the virtue of responsibility, that rewards responsibility, and punishes irresponsibility.

The Entitlement State fosters a growing entitlement mentality, where unwary Americans support "free" healthcare, or where fast food workers demand a "living wage" far in excess of the federal minimum wage and/or what their skills can justify.

Now is the time, not to save Social Security and the Entitlement State, but to dismantle it.

- - - - - -

In next month's newsletter, we will share some additional excerpts on how we can transform Social Security and begin to re-establish a Self-Reliant Society.

US Debt Clock - - March 1st - $56,615 per citizen / April 1st - $56,674

Newsletter No. 17   May 2015

In this month's newsletter, we share some additional excerpts from Don Watkins' book entitled *RooseveltCare* (How Social Security is Sabotaging the Land of Self-Reliance) -

Self-reliant Americans eagerly pursued their own interest in concert with others by means of each person's voluntary participation in families, communities, schools, and civic organizations. The American soul was a mixture of self-reliance and selfless service to others. America had an abundant system of private charity. [Unfortunately, this has now been replaced by the Entitlement State].

The century leading up to the passage of Social Security in 1935 would do more to relieve poverty and increase life's security than any prior century in human history.

Social Security does not just "redistribute" wealth, it drastically reduces how much wealth is produced in the first place. It is not zero-sum - - it is negative-sum. When welfare state spending took off during the late 1960s, this is when America's poverty rate stopped declining. This shouldn't come as a surprise. When the welfare state transfers money away from the people who create it, it undermines how much wealth gets produced in the first place. The Entitlement State did not end poverty – it reduced prosperity. Poverty is not a distribution problem, it is a production problem. The Entitlement State has made each of us far poorer than we would otherwise be.

The best analogy for Social Security's Trust Fund is to think of parents who set aside their child's college fund in a jar, but who periodically "borrow" from the jar whenever they want to go on vacation, etc, and replace the cash with an IOU. By the time the child is ready to go to college, the jar is full of IOUs, which will not do a thing to help the parents pay for their child's schooling.

The government can print green pieces of paper at will. But it cannot bring new wealth into existence by fiat.

In July 2013, rock singer Bono made headlines when he said, "Aid is just a stop-gap. Commerce and entrepreneurial capitalism take more people out of poverty than aid."

The self-reliant person views productive work, not as a dreary duty, but as an avenue for prosperity, creativity, growth, fulfillment, pride, and joy. He / she does not envy the fact that others may achieve more than they do. His / her chief financial goal is independence.

The Founding Fathers took a crucial leap forward, by declaring that the collective has no claim on you; that the government exists only to protect your right to live your own life.

A self-reliant society nurtures freedom, justice, opportunity and prosperity. We must drop the platitude that the goals of the Entitlement State are "noble" - - those goals are un-American.

I am not my grandfather's keeper. Parents do not steal from their children.

- - - -

Mr. Watkins ends his book with a chapter on how we can abolish the Entitlement State. He encourages us to distribute his book to our friends and family. He asks "What are our chances of success? And on what time scale? If you know that a course of action is right, and there is a chance you can win, then you fight, regardless of the odds, and regardless of how long it will take." Our Editorial Board whole-heartedly agrees.

US Debt Clock - - April 1st - $56,674 per citizen / May 1st - $56,725

Newsletter No. 18   June 2015

Here is an interesting question about the Entitlement State - - What about medical care? Doesn't the Declaration of Independence mention an inalienable right to life (etc)? So, doesn't that mean the government is required to provide healthcare? (The original answer to that question was "No").

Unfortunately, over the intervening years since our country's founding, a number of "progressive" presidents (such as Woodrow Wilson, FDR and LBJ) felt that the government needed to have (additional) powers to do whatever the progressives thought the "national interest" required.

The reason the Entitlement State is an *un-American* concept is that it was based on the belief that regular US citizens were incapable of managing their own personal lives. Therefore, it was up to the government to establish a program that would provide a retirement benefit for every citizen (not just for those elderly retirees who might otherwise need to rely on their family members, or turn to a charitable/civic organization for assistance).

But isn't healthcare different? The answer is still "No". Otherwise, that line of thinking would lead you to a conclusion that the federal government is also obligated to provide you with food and housing, too. Having said that... Our Editorial Board does believe that it is OK for the government to have a regulatory oversight (protection) role in regards to healthcare issues. One of the primary reasons Medicare came into existence in the 1960s is that insurance companies were reluctant to provide a health insurance policy to an elderly person with significant medical issues. However, the unfortunate consequence was a massive expansion of the federal bureaucracy to manage the country's healthcare system.

The Entitlement State is one of the major drivers of the country's annual deficit and cumulative debt. The country's entitlement programs need to be reformed / transformed, because there are now fewer than three workers for each retiree. The annual deficit amounts for Medicare and Social Security are projected to continually increase each year, and the projected deficits for Medicare are even larger than the amounts for Social Security.

Our Editorial Board would like to see the restoration of commonsense regulation of the country's healthcare system, by devolving it back to the states. The country's private healthcare industry (which is a "regulated industry" at the state level) should continue to be the primary healthcare delivery system for the vast majority of the country's citizens. In regards to the elderly (and "welfare-eligible" citizens) we feel that it is OK for the federal government to establish appropriate, minimum national standards (i.e., the rules and regulations). In addition, it is OK for the federal government to collect "Medical Care" payroll taxes, but those funds should immediately be refunded directly back to the applicable state for its healthcare program. It should be up to the US House of Representatives and US Senate to determine each year how much additional financial assistance the federal government should provide to each state to support each state's healthcare program. The role of the federal government should be changed from a "management" (bureaucracy) role, to an "advisory / regulatory oversight" role.

US Debt Clock - - May 1st - $56,725 per citizen / June 1st - $56,860

Newsletter No. 19   July 2015

In last month's newsletter we asked whether the "inalienable right to life" means the federal government is obligated to provide healthcare to the country's citizens. Our Editorial Board continues to believe that the answer to this question is "No" - and the management of the country's healthcare system is not an appropriate role of the federal government. Unfortunately, the size and scope of the Entitlement State continues to grow. And unfortunately, the Supreme Court has ruled that the country's taxpayers must provide subsidies so that all citizens (including those who qualify for subsidies) can fulfill their "individual mandate" requirement under Obamacare.

But aren't healthcare and welfare benefits an obligation of the federal government (as mentioned in the introduction to the US Constitution - - *We the People of the United States, in order to form a more perfect union, … to promote the general welfare…*) ?? Our Editorial Board believes that the answer to the welfare question is also "No". The "general welfare" clause means the federal government has a general obligation to the country as a whole. It does not have an obligation to provide for the daily needs of each individual citizen, which is a Personal Responsibility.

So, what role should the federal government play in regards to welfare benefits? Our Editorial Board's position is "basically none". The federal government's primary role is to protect the country as a whole, and effectively manage the relationships between our country and other countries in the world. It should have an outward (rather than inward) focus. Social services for individual citizens are much more effectively delivered at the local level, rather than by a government bureaucracy. We feel that welfare assistance is more effectively provided by Not-for-Profit charitable organizations, which are vastly superior to the federal government (or a state government) in the delivery of social services to people who need assistance.

As the federal government's size and scope has grown over the years, one of the unfortunate side effects has been a reduction in the citizens' financial support to these key civic / charitable organizations. This has happened because people have been led to believe that "the government" was going to solve the problem(s). However, the federal government's War on Poverty, which began in the 1960s, has not achieved any measurable positive results. In fact, once the War on Poverty began, the percentage of people living in poverty stopped declining. The federal government's welfare system has failed the poor.

The government has already spent roughly $22 trillion dollars on the War on Poverty since the 1960s (which exceeds the amount the government has spent on all military wars combined since the beginning of our nation's history). President Obama's proposed budget continues to advocate for this broken system, and recommends that the government spend another $13 trillion on means-tested welfare programs during the next ten years. We believe the federal government is the wrong entity to try to eliminate poverty. Social services delivered by Not-for-Profit charitable organizations prove to be much more effective in helping the poor become self-sufficient.

Our Editorial Board believes that in order to re-establish a self-reliant society, the federal government's policies should be geared towards supporting the family unit and promoting Personal Responsibility. We believe the federal income tax code should be revised to help achieve appropriate levels of financial support to qualified Not-for-Profit charitable organizations (rather than have the funds diverted to another government welfare program).

US Debt Clock - - June 1st - $56,860 per citizen / July 1st - $56,943

Newsletter No. 20   August 2015

As we have discussed in the last few newsletters, our Editorial Board has shared a number of recommendations on how our country can move forward to Fix the Debt. In this newsletter, we would like to direct you to our Foundation's website (F2PPR.org) and the Join the Conversation page. We have added a new conversation piece entitled *The 2020 Initiative*

http://www.f2ppr.org/wp-content/uploads/2016/06/The-2020-Initiative.pdf

which discusses six highly inter-related issues that must be addressed in order for our country to resolve the growing debt problem. The six issues are Fiscal Responsibility, Term Limits, Tax Reform, Welfare Reform, Social Security Reform, and Medicare/healthcare Reform.

Over the past several months, our Editorial Board members have shared these recommendations with a number of our country's elected officials and with many of the candidates who are running for president. We have emphasized that in order to successfully begin re-paying the country's outstanding debt, each of these six inter-related proposals would need to be implemented. Implementing only three of the six, or even five of the six, will not serve to accomplish the goal of paying off the country's debt.

The first order of business is to have our country's elected leaders acknowledge that pushing the country's growing debt problem onto future generations is immoral. It will take true leadership (along with political compromise and bipartisan cooperation) to achieve fiscal responsibility and start repaying the country's outstanding debt over the course of the next few generations. Our Editorial Board agrees with the following assertions by the Campaign to Fix the Debt –

The solution(s) to the country's debt problem will need to include both spending reductions and increases in tax revenues.

Everyone in the country will need to make sacrifices and "give up something".

The country is in a deep $18.3 trillion hole. Therefore, the first step needs to be "stop the bleeding" and reduce the annual deficit amount to zero. Even this first step will be extremely difficult to achieve. It will entail a significant transformation of our country - - away from the Entitlement State and away from "business as usual" in our nation's capitol. We must begin to implement reforms to the country's entitlement programs. Many of our recommendations represent a fairly radical change to the existing programs. But we can no longer delay. The country's debt problem will not magically disappear overnight - - we must begin to act now.

It should be noted that no one (including the diverse members of our Editorial Board) will be in complete agreement with all aspects of these six recommendations. As we noted above, everyone is going to have to give up something if we are ever going to be able to move forward on the country's debt issue. Everyone will naturally want someone else to pay to fix the problem. We are putting forward *The 2020 Initiative* as a set of inter-related changes that should be implemented, so that the country can return to a Self-Reliant Society, where We-the-People again promote Personal Responsibility, rather than rely on another government program.

US Debt Clock - - July 1st - $56,943 per citizen / August 1st - $57,032

Newsletter No. 21   September 2015

Many of our recent newsletters have covered the creation (and subsequent expansion) of the "Entitlement State". Unfortunately, the first step that our federal government took on this road towards fiscal irresponsibility started in 1935 with the "unfunded pension benefits" created under the Social Security program. We should keep in mind that this program was established with the best of intentions, which was to create a government program that would help keep elderly retirees out of poverty. However, the program provides an entitlement benefit to nearly all US citizens, without regard to a person's / family's financial needs during retirement. This is the fundamental flaw of the Social Security program.

In this month's newsletter, we would again like to direct you to our Foundation's website (F2PPR.org) and the Join the Conversation page, where we have posted "A Letter to Senator Bernie Sanders regarding Social Security" -

http://www.f2ppr.org/wp-content/uploads/2013/11/A-Letter-to-Senator-Bernie-Sanders-regarding-Social-Security.pdf

The letter discusses five "hypothetical" US citizens, their working careers and total wages, and the resulting amounts that they receive from Social Security.

As the letter points out, most of the scenarios do not make any sense (at all). A "Barely Eligible Recipient" who earned minimal wages for the minimum number of years needed to qualify for Social Security would receive a monthly benefit of $112 per month, or $1,344 per year. We believe that if this person doesn't have any other financial means, they are probably someone who would need to receive assistance from the government or a charitable organization, but they aren't getting much from Social Security.

Conversely, a hypothetical "Upper Middle Class Recipient" who earned wages equal to the Social Security wage cap each year (a total of $2.7 million) would receive $601,692 in Social Security benefits during their retirement, which is an amount that exceeds their contributions into the program by $433,591. This individual receives 3.6 times as much as they paid into Social Security. What's even worse is that a "Very Well Off Recipient" who made twice the Social Security wage cap (a total of $5.4 million) would also receive $601,692 in Social Security benefits. So, here is the fundamental question - Why does the federal government pay pension benefits (and relatively higher amounts) to "financially secure" people who probably don't need to receive these payments?

Our Editorial Board believes the reason that 8 out of 10 people think Social Security is such a great program is that many of our country's citizens get back more than five times the amount they pay into the system. However, another way to look at Social Security (and any other "entitlement" program) is that our country's citizens are being bribed with our money. What's even worse is that (in reality) it is our children's and grandchildren's money, because there is no actual cash in the Social Security "Trust" (only intergovernmental IOUs). All of our payroll tax withholdings have already been spent (along with another $18.3 trillion that the government has borrowed against future generations).

As we recommend in *The 2020 Initiative*, Social Security should be transformed over a multi-year transition period into a means-tested welfare benefit. Eventually, these unfunded pensions should be phased out, and a "financial security" welfare benefit should only be paid to those elderly retirees who need assistance. Otherwise, this program will continue to steal huge sums of money from our children and grandchildren.

US Debt Clock - - August 1st - $57,032 per citizen / September 1st - $57,120

Newsletter No. 22   October 2015

In this month's newsletter, we were originally going to provide an update on the ongoing dysfunction occurring in our nation's capitol now that Congress has returned from their August recess, and now that the federal government's new fiscal year has begun on October 1st - - No budget for the upcoming year, Congress passing a short-term "Continuing Resolution" that merely pushes off the next round of the same problem until December 11th, No action on entitlement reform, No action on the country's debt ceiling, etc., etc. However, we recently ran across an interesting Associated Press article with the headline "Household Wealth Reaches New High", and we thought that we should share some of this information with you instead, and we could help put some of this information into perspective.

The article reported on a recently released Federal Reserve report that disclosed the Fed's latest estimates of US households' assets and liabilities as of the second quarter of 2015. The article was basically a "feel good" piece, which stated that the wealth of US households has recovered over the past several years and has risen to a new high of $85.7 trillion, and "rising household wealth can help boost growth by making consumers feel wealthier and more likely to spend."

We have included the following link to the Federal Reserve's report - http://www.federalreserve.gov/releases/z1/current/z1.pdf

Here are some of the key amounts - - Total Household Assets - $100 trillion, Total Household Liabilities - $14.3 trillion, which equals US Households' Net Worth (Wealth) - $85.7 trillion.

The Federal Reserve's report contains some interesting details, but the report was more interesting for what it failed to include. Total Household Assets include $69.8 trillion of "financial assets" (with the details shown for bank accounts, stocks, bonds, treasury securities, mutual funds, etc.) and $30.2 trillion of non-financial assets (the largest amount being real estate). The $14.3 trillion of Total Household Liabilities primarily consist of $9.4 trillion for home mortgages and $3.3 trillion for consumer credit (credit cards, student loans, etc).

What we found interesting is that in determining the wealth of US households, the Federal Reserve includes treasury securities in US households' financial assets, but fails to include the US households' $18 trillion liability for the cumulative US debt that has been incurred by our federal government. In our opinion, the US Households' Net Worth of $85.7 trillion should be reduced by 21% to show the effect of this liability. The US debt incurred by our federal government (on our collective behalf) exceeds the amount of liabilities that have been directly, consciously incurred by US households.

Maybe some fairy godmother is going to come along and make this $18 trillion liability magically disappear. (We suspect not). So maybe the Federal Reserve and Associated Press should make a note that in future press releases they should communicate all of the pertinent facts to our country's citizens.

US Debt Clock - - September 1st - $57,120 per citizen / October 1st - $57,150

Newsletter No. 23   November 2015
Bernie Sanders is right (and also very wrong)
Opportunity for All, Favoritism to None

Last week the US House of Representatives and US Senate passed legislation to (again) suspend the country's debt ceiling, choosing to kick the can down the road, this time until March 2017. In effect, our elected representatives have decided that fiscal responsibility can wait until after the presidential election next November.

As the country's two major political parties begin hosting their presidential candidate debates, the fundamental differences between the two parties are coming into focus. During the initial Democratic debate on October 13th, Senator Bernie Sanders highlighted a couple of very important issues about the country's political situation, and he is absolutely right –

"There is a profound frustration with Establishment Politics"

"The government is involved in our emails... is involved in our websites.... Yes, we have to defend ourselves against terrorism, but there are many ways to do this without impinging on our constitutional rights and our privacy rights."

Our Editorial Board agrees with Senator Sanders that the level of frustration with Establishment Politics is growing, and this is borne out by a number of statistics. Congress' approval rating has continued to be stuck in the low teens for the past several years. More than half of the country's citizens disapprove of President Obama's job performance. More than half of the country's citizens disapprove of the Supreme Court's performance. But the most alarming statistic is the growing level of voter apathy. As Senator Sanders noted during the debate, 63% of eligible voters did not go to the polls during the 2014 mid-term elections. The level of voter participation continues to drop each election cycle. So the questions remain – If not us, who? If not now, when?

Our Editorial Board also shares Senator Sanders' concern about the infringement on our citizens' constitutional rights by an ever-expanding federal government. However, Senator Sanders stated that his primary concern is not necessarily the large federal government, but the country's billionaire class and large corporations (which happen to be the source of many of our citizens' better paying jobs). We agree with Senator Sanders that we need to continue to address the issue of influence peddling, and we need to guard against any favoritism that the federal government doles out to any corporation, or to any labor union, or to any other special interest group (any "sub-segment" of the population). However, our Editorial Board is much more concerned about the protection of our citizens' rights, and the possibility of our country being damaged by our massive, ever-expanding federal government and our country's growing debt problem.

Unfortunately, neither Senator Sanders (nor any of the other Democratic candidates) made any mention of the need for the federal government to exercise fiscal responsibility. It should be noted that this "oversight" might have been by design, because none of the debate moderators ever raised any questions about the cumulative US debt, and none of the candidates put forward any solutions on how we can begin repaying the country's $18.4 trillion debt. Interestingly, the only time the word "debt" was uttered during the debate was during discussions about how the federal government should implement a new social program to help a sub-segment of the population pay off their student loan debt. Instead of discussing the need for smaller, better-managed government, Senator Sanders proposed several new social programs, such as "free" college tuition, an expansion of Social Security benefits, and an even larger federal government.

So what does our country need to do, to reverse the growth in federal government spending? We have added two new Conversation Pieces to our F2PPR.org website –

http://www.f2ppr.org/wp-content/uploads/2015/10/Fair-versus-Unfortunate.pdf

http://www.f2ppr.org/wp-content/uploads/2015/10/A-Right-versus-A-Personal-Responsibility.pdf

US Debt Clock - - October 1st - $57,150 per citizen / November 1st - $57,203

The Republican Presidential Candidates' Debates

First, an update... As we mentioned last month, our elected representatives in Washington DC have passed legislation to (again) suspend the country's debt ceiling until March 2017. As part of that legislative "success" our representatives gave themselves a deadline of December 11th to pass spending appropriation bills for the federal government's fiscal year that began on October 1st. We will give you another update next month.

The Republican presidential candidates held their third and fourth debates on October 28th in Boulder, Colorado, and November 10th in Milwaukee, Wisconsin. Many of the candidates discussed some of the spending and other fiscal challenges facing the country -

Chris Christie - Let me be honest with the people who are watching at home. The government has lied to you and they have stolen from you. They told you that your Social Security money is in a trust fund. All that is in that trust fund is a pile of IOUs for money they spent on something else a long time ago.... 71% of federal spending today is on entitlements and debt service.

Bobby Jindal - We keep stealing from our children. That is immoral. That is wrong, and we are creating more government dependents....   Barack Obama has done a lot of damage to our country. I think one of the worst things he has done is try to change the idea of America to be one of dependence.

Ted Cruz - ....the current [tax] system isn't fair. Washington is fundamentally corrupt. Every page [of the tax code] reflects a carve-out or a subsidy, and it is all about empowering the Washington cartel.

Carly Fiorina - This is how Socialism starts. Government causes a problem, and then government steps in to "solve" the problem. This is why we need to take our government back.

Marco Rubio - This election is about the future. The Left and the Democratic Party have no idea about the future. All of their ideas are the same tired ideas of the past - more government, more spending. For every issue before America, their answer is a new tax on someone, and a new government program.

Jeb Bush - Hillary Clinton has said that Barack Obama's policies get an "A". Really? One in ten people right now aren't working or have given up altogether. That is not an "A". One in seven are living in poverty. That is not an "A". One in five children are on food stamps. That is not an "A". It may be the best that Hillary Clinton can do, but that is not the best that America can do.

Rand Paul – This is the unholy alliance that people need to know about between the Right and Left. The Right and Left are spending us into oblivion. We are borrowing $1 million a minute... We have to ask the question – Where is money best spent - in the private sector or in the government sector?.... Liberty thrives when government is small. I want a government so small you can barely see it.

Mike Huckabee – I've got five grandkids. I do not want to walk my five grandkids through the charred remains of a once-great country called America, and say "Here you go. $20 trillion of debt. Good luck making something out of this mess".

Marco Rubio – Washington is out of touch through the fault of both political parties... We have a $19 trillion bipartisan debt.... If the next four years are anything like the last eight years, our children will be the first Americans ever left worse off by their parents.

-   -   -   -   -

Our Editorial Board agrees that next year's presidential election represents a clear choice between an ever-expanding federal government, or taking back our government from the Washington cartel. Our government needs to support policies that promote Personal Responsibility and provide Opportunity for All. Our government needs to stop showing any favoritism to special interest groups, and end crony capitalism. And we need to stop stealing from our children and grandkids. If not us, who? If not now, when?

Best wishes for a happy holiday season, and a brighter 2016. We can get this fixed.

US Debt Clock - - November 1st - $57,203 per citizen / December 1st - $58,060

Newsletter No. 25   January 2016
Favoritism to Many Special Interest Groups

We hope that everyone had a happy holiday season. For a lot of people, Christmas came one week early this year. On December 18th, the US House of Representatives and US Senate passed a massive (2,009 page) spending and "tax extenders" bill, which paired two pieces of legislation – a $1.15 trillion spending bill and a bill that contains a number of provisions that affect the taxation of businesses and individuals. Some pundits have opined that the primary benefit of this legislative "success" was that it enabled the federal government to remain open, and the full faith and credit of the government was left intact. The reality is that much of this spending should not have been approved, and the full faith and credit of the federal government has taken yet another hit because of this legislation.

The "omnibus" appropriations bill funds all of the government's agencies for the current fiscal year that began on October 1st. Keep in mind that this $1.15 trillion of spending represents the "non-mandatory" portion of federal spending (29% of the total). The remaining 71% of the government's cash outflows was not even addressed by this spending bill, because that portion of the federal government's spending is for debt service and for "entitlements" that are on automatic pilot, using formulas that career politicians do not have the courage and/or will to change.

Congress also passed the Protecting Americans from Tax Hikes (PATH) Act, which extended various tax breaks, preferences, deductions and credits. Unfortunately, with the 2016 deficit already budgeted to be in excess of $470 billion, our elected representatives felt a need to "protect" us from tax hikes. But what we really need is protection from any further spending increases. The total cost of these "tax expenditures" (lost tax revenues) is estimated to be in excess of $622 billion over the next ten years. Some estimates put the cost as high as $680 billion.

The tax breaks for certain sub-segments of the country's citizens include residential energy conservation credits, teachers' classroom expense deductions, "transit benefits" for mass transit and parking benefits, the child tax credit, the earned income credit, qualified tuition deductions and other education credits, but no "free" college education (yet).

The tax breaks for certain select businesses (the beneficiaries of crony capitalism) include special rules and tax preferences for the biofuels industry, wind energy, alternative fuel / fuel cell vehicles, real estate investment trusts, restaurants, film and television producers, motorsports complexes, race horses, mine safety equipment, railroad track maintenance, etc., etc.

An Associated Press release was issued the day after this legislation was signed into law. The final sentence summed it up fairly well – "Congress' top leaders of both parties took turns claiming credit for the holiday-season largesse." It's probably safe to say that many of our country's citizens are excited by the thought of all of this "free money" being doled out by the federal government. But the truth of the matter is the Washington cartel has once again hit future generations with a double-whammy. The appropriations bill busts the spending caps that Congress approved in 2011, and Congress continues to dole out tax breaks to special interest groups (both favored businesses and select sub-segments of the country's citizens).

US Debt Clock - - December 1st - $58,060 per citizen / January 1st - $58,268

Newsletter No. 26 February 2016
Left and Right Differences

The 2016 presidential election cycle has officially begun with the onset of the Iowa caucuses. In making our selection of the country's next president, it is very important for We-the-People to assess the "personality" and trustworthiness of each of the candidates (Donald / Hillary). However, we believe that it is more important to listen to the candidates' views on the role of the federal government, their priorities if they were to be elected, and their proposals on how to deal with the key issues that should be addressed during the election.

In this regard, we believe that it is very important to understand the fundamental differences between the two political parties. We have included the following link, which will take you to five five-minute videos that highlight the key differences between the Left ("Progressives") and the Right ("Conservatives").

https://www.prageru.com/courses/left-and-right-differences

If you only have time to view one of these videos, we recommend the first video - *How Big Should Government Be?* It discusses seven inevitable outcomes that result from an ever-expanding government. It concludes with the following observation – Without the belief in an ever-expanding government, there is no Left. Without a belief in limited government, there is no Right.

We also like # 2 – *Does it Feel Good or Does it Do Good?* It asks a fundamental question - Does a particular government policy or program do good (for society) or does it just make you feel good (about yourself)? We need to remember that the highway to hell is oftentimes paved with the best of intentions.

And then there is # 5 – *How Do We Make Society Better?* This one might be the best of the five. It explains that Conservatives believe the way to a better society is almost always through the moral improvement of the individual; by each person doing battle with his or her own weaknesses and flaws (and assuming Personal Responsibility). On the other hand, Progressives are pre-occupied with using the power of the government to fix the moral failings of "society".

We also want to let you know that we have included a new conversation piece on the Foundation's website. Thomas Paine was one of the country's Founders, and in 1776, he wrote a pamphlet entitled *Common Sense* -

http://www.f2ppr.org/wp-content/uploads/2016/01/Thomas-Paine-and-Common-Sense.pdf

Many of these self-evident truths are just as true today as they were back in 1776.

US Debt Clock - - January 1st - $58,268 per citizen / February 1st - $58,727

Newsletter No. 27   March 2016
Our Attempt to Define "Fairness"

During the Democratic Party presidential candidates' debates, there has been a lot of talk about how the amount of taxes paid by the country's wealthiest citizens is not enough, and that they should pay their "fair share". Unfortunately, none of the candidates have specifically defined what amount or level of taxes would be fair (only that it's not enough). And unfortunately, with the Left's (Progressives') spending plans, it appears that no amount could ever possibly be high enough. And unfortunately, we cannot even afford our current level of spending, so the federal government continues to rely on annual deficits and an increasing amount of debt that is being pushed onto future generations.

We have included the following link to an interesting five-minute video that attempts to answer the question of whether the rich pay their fair share of taxes.

https://www.prageru.com/courses/economics/do-rich-pay-their-fair-share

The question has two parts – who is rich? and what is fair? Contrary to many people on the Left, our Editorial Board members are not envious of successful people. (We applaud successful people). believe that our country's citizens should be free to make as much money as they can (or want to) as long as they are not doing anything that is illegal.

So the question is - What is "fair" (for everybody - now AND in the future). The video puts forward one possible answer - that the portion of the population that makes 10% of the country's income should pay 10% of the country's taxes, and that the portion of the population that makes 20% of the country's income should pay 20% of the country's taxes, and so on. We disagree with this simplistic answer, because we feel that each American citizen should strive to be a self-reliant person, and no individual / family should pay federal income taxes until they have earned an amount that is at least equal to the applicable federal poverty guideline amount. We also believe that progressive income tax rates continue to be appropriate (at least for the near future) and that tax rates should not be decreased until the country's cumulative debt amount has been repaid.

The video also discusses payroll taxes for Social Security and Medicare. Unfortunately, it does not discuss the fact that an employee's wages are first taxed for Social Security and Medicare, and then those wages are taxed again for federal income tax purposes. The video also does not discuss whether these socialistic programs should ever have been implemented to begin with, because they represent an over-reach by the federal government, and they are no longer affordable (as currently constituted) due to changes in the country's demographics. It is immoral that we, as a country, have pushed the financial obligation for these programs onto future generations. These programs need to be fundamentally transformed over a multi-year transition period, and the payroll taxes that are paid each year for these programs should count towards satisfying a portion of a person's / family's total tax obligation for the year.

Hillary Clinton has said that if she were to be elected, she would not increase taxes on any family making less than $250,000 per year. So how is she going to eliminate deficit spending, begin to repay the country's debt, and raise enough taxes to pay for the new programs that she is proposing? Well... She (or Bernie Sanders) is simply going to get the money from the Top 1%. However, as noted in another Prager University video entitled *"How to Solve America's Spending Problem"* increasing the amount of taxes on the Top 1% is not a sufficient (or viable) answer. The amount of the deficit that is projected for the current fiscal year in President Obama's latest budget is $616 billion (another $2,000 per citizen). Even if the federal government were to take 100% of the earnings of everyone who makes more than $1 million, this would only raise federal tax revenues by $600 billion, so this wouldn't even get us out of the hole for the current year. Pandering career politicians (in both parties) have never been any good at simple math, nor at being straightforward with the country's citizens. It is true that the federal government could go ahead and take this action, and within a few years, the number of viable businesses in the country would decrease significantly (and the number of employees who earn a living wage would also decrease significantly). We cannot tax ourselves into prosperity.

Our Editorial Board believes that the only thing that is "fair" is to have each citizen assume Personal Responsibility for their own life (including their own food, shelter, utilities, continuing education, healthcare, retirement, etc.). The federal government needs to reverse course, and stop trying to assume all of the roles that properly reside with civil society. We need to shrink the size of the federal government, and have it re-focus on its responsibilities that were laid out in the Constitution. Common Sense tells us that these self-evident truths are just as true today as they were back in 1776.

US Debt Clock - - February 1st - $58,727 per citizen / March 1st - $58,980

Newsletter No. 28   April 2016
The Role of the federal government

Last month we put forward a radical idea - - the federal government should stop trying to assume all of the roles that properly reside with the states, or with civil society, or with the individual. The Tenth Amendment in the Bill of Rights states that *The powers not delegated to the United States by the Constitution, nor prohibited by it to the States, are reserved to the States respectively, or to the people.* Our Editorial Board believes the federal government should re-focus its attention towards its responsibilities that were specified in the US Constitution.

However, the Progressives' agenda is that the federal government should grow to assume whatever responsibility(s) the federal government deems that it should have. So the real question becomes, what is the proper role of the federal government? We have included the following link to the applicable section of the US Constitution (Article 1, Section 8) that lists the responsibilities of the federal government -

http://www.f2ppr.org/wp-content/uploads/2016/03/The-US-Constitution-Article-1-Section-8.pdf

As you read through the list, it is readily apparent that there is one common theme – the federal government's primary role is one of protection - to protect the general welfare of the country as a whole, and to protect the rights of the country's citizens.

The first sentence sets forth the responsibility to provide for the common defense of the country. Section 8 goes on to make references to the country's army, navy, militias, forts, arsenals, and dockyards.

The federal government's responsibilities also include establishing tribunals (courts) to protect the citizens' rights.

The specific language that was used by the Founders is interesting to note - for example, *"To promote the progress of science and useful arts, by securing for limited times to authors and inventors the exclusive right to their respective writings and discoveries."* Again, the role of the government is to protect the rights of individual citizens. This sentence does not say that the federal government has the responsibility to make progress in science and the useful arts (although the supporters of the Progressive agenda would disagree).

It should be noted that our Editorial Board does disagree with one of the responsibilities that was originally listed in the Constitution - - it is time to privatize the US Post Office. There is no longer any reason for the federal government to run the Post Office (and lose billions of dollars each year while it mis-manages what is essentially a business operation).

The government is also responsible for providing punishment for any counterfeiting of the country's currency. The government needs to protect the value of our currency (and it shouldn't debase the value of our currency by borrowing $19 trillion of debt to be repaid by future generations).

The federal government is also responsible "To regulate commerce with foreign nations." As we have noted elsewhere on our website, our Editorial Board believes the focus of the federal government should be directed outwards - - towards our country's relationships with other countries around the world. Unfortunately, the liberal / progressive agenda serves to distract the attention of the federal government away from this fundamental role, and instead distracts the federal government with a focus on "internal" domestic issues that should be dealt with by the states, civil society, families, or by the people themselves (i.e., Personal Responsibilities). Common Sense tells us that these self-evident truths are just as true today as they were back in 1776.

US Debt Clock - - March 1st - $58,980 per citizen / April 1st - $59,420

Newsletter No. 29   **May 2016**
The US Constitution – An Opportunity to Learn More

Last month we provided a link to Article 1, Section 8 of the US Constitution, which lists the responsibilities of the federal government. Nowhere in the Constitution does it mention that the federal government should provide healthcare to all of the country's citizens (or food or housing), or provide a monthly pension benefit to a retired citizen.

So, how did we start heading down this long and winding road towards socialism and an ever-expanding federal government and a cumulative debt of $19.3 trillion? The simplistic answer is that Article 1, Section 8 gives to Congress the responsibility *To make all Laws which shall be necessary and proper....* But unfortunately, the supporters of the liberal/progressive agenda fail to read the entire sentence - *To make all Laws which shall be necessary and proper for carrying into Execution the foregoing Powers* – (the powers that are listed above this sentence in Section 8).

On our website, we have a Conversation Piece entitled *"Don't Tread on Me" / There Ought to be a Law (or Not)*. The Founders of our country established a federal government with limited powers, and with the intent that the federal government would focus on a few vital functions, which are primarily oriented towards protecting the country as a whole and the citizens' rights. Unfortunately, over the course of time (and due to some of our elected officials' desire to "fix a problem" or advance a favor towards a special interest group or some other sub-segment of the population) we now have a federal income tax code (including IRS Regulations and Official Guidance) that is in excess of 70,000 pages and 4 million words. We also have a situation where it is easy for a citizen to commit three crimes a day, oftentimes without knowing it. (We recommend that you do an internet search on a book entitled *Three Felonies a Day* by Boston civil rights lawyer Harvey Silverglate).

Fortunately, it is possible to get off the road that we're heading down, if we simply return to the Founders' idea of Limited Government. And fortunately, there is an educational institution that has created a series of online courses that gives everyone an opportunity to better understand our country's founding principles. The following link takes you to Hillsdale College's website and the page that lists the various courses that are available (for free) -

http://online.hillsdale.edu/dashboard/courses

The course entitled *Introduction to the Constitution* is a good place to start, to refresh your understanding of representative government, the separation of powers, and the principles of Limited Government. The fourth segment of this course highlights the differences between centralized, bureaucratic rule and constitutional government.

Constitution 101 – The Meaning & History of the Constitution will provide you with a more in-depth understanding of the underlying principles behind our country's founding. It includes a segment on The Progressives' Rejection of the Principles of the Declaration of Independence, along with The Progressives' Assault on the Constitution.

Lastly, we also highly recommend *Constitution 201*, which includes a segment entitled *Restoring Constitutional Government*. Common Sense tells us that the principles behind Limited Government are just as true today as they were back in the 1700s.

US Debt Clock - - April 1st - $59,420 per citizen / May 1st - $59,558

Newsletter No. 30   June 2016
Benefiting from the wisdom of others

Just a short newsletter this month.

On our website's Home Page, we mentioned that one of our Foundation's primary objectives is to share with our readers some of the wisdom from our country's founders and other influential thought leaders. We have added a new Conversation Piece on our website, where we have posted a collection of quotes about Personal Responsibility, the federal government, and other topics. Here is the link -

http://www.f2ppr.org/wp-content/uploads/2016/05/Pearls-of-Wisdom.pdf

We hold these truths to be self-evident.

US Debt Clock - - May 1st - $59,558 per citizen / June 1st - $59,569

Newsletter No. 31   July 2016
A platform for The Party of Personal Freedom

In a few weeks, both major political parties will hold their conventions - - the Republicans in Cleveland on July 18-21, and the Democrats in Philadelphia on July 25-28. Unfortunately, once the parties' conventions are over, our country's citizens will be subjected to several months of negative television commercials regarding the personality and trustworthiness of the two major parties' presidential candidates.

Our Editorial Board agrees that the trustworthiness of the individuals who are running for president is an important issue. However, we believe it is even more important that our country's citizens have a constructive conversation about the underlying principles of the two major political parties regarding the size and scope and proper role of the federal government. To that end, we have added a new Conversation Piece on our website that puts forward a platform that would move the country towards a new and better "desired state" - - the Founders' original idea of limited government. Let's call it the platform of The Party of Personal Freedom –

http://www.f2ppr.org/wp-content/uploads/2016/06/The-Party-of-Personal-Freedom.pdf

We believe the most important question for the 2016 election is - - Do we want an even bigger, constantly expanding, more intrusive federal government? Or do we want individual liberties and personal freedom?

US Debt Clock - - June 1st - $59,569 per citizen / July 1st - $59,640

Newsletter No. 32   August 2016
Seven Inevitable Results

The Republican and Democratic parties' conventions are over, and the mudslinging has begun in earnest - an unfortunate, inevitable result of our country's political process. But our Editorial Board would like to keep the focus on the parties' principles, rather than the personalities and trustworthiness of individual candidates. The two parties' platforms are available on the internet at –

https://prod-static-ngop-pbl.s3.amazonaws.com/media/documents/DRAFT_12_FINAL[1]-ben_1468872234.pdf   and

https://www.democrats.org/party-platform

Our Editorial Board was somewhat disappointed by the GOP platform, because it attempts to make a case for supporting certain initiatives (such as advancing responsible homeownership) that are beyond the scope of the federal government's responsibilities spelled out in the Constitution.

The Democrats' platform is extremely disturbing - - the Table of Contents is a three-page laundry list of "social engineering" progressive initiatives that are well beyond the scope of the federal government's responsibilities, and several are counter-productive programs that will inevitably lead to unintended consequences.

In our February newsletter, we provided a link to a website that contains several 5-minute videos that highlight the key differences between the Left ("Progressives") and the Right ("Conservatives"). The following link is to the video that discusses seven inevitable results that arise from Big Government –

https://www.prageru.com/courses/left-and-right-differences/how-big-should-government-be-left-vs-right-1

1. There will be ever increasing amounts of corruption. [Power and money breed corruption.]

2. Individual liberty will decline.

3. Countries with ever-expanding governments will either reduce the size of their government, or eventually collapse economically.

4. In order to pay for an ever-expanding government, taxes are constantly increased.

5. Big Government produces big deficits and ever-increasing and ultimately unsustainable debt.

6. The bigger the government, the greater the opportunities for doing great evil. [Coca Cola cannot break into your house or confiscate your wealth, or build concentration camps, or commit genocide. Only Big Governments can do that.]

7. Big Government eats away at the moral character of a nation. [People no longer take care of other people. They (erroneously) think "the government" will take care of that.]

The Left believes the state should be the most powerful force in society - - not parents, not businesses, not private schools, not religious institutions, not even the individual human conscience. Without the belief in an ever-expanding government, there is no Left. Without a belief in limited government, there is no Right.

US Debt Clock - - July 1st - $59,640 per citizen / August 1st - $59,899

Newsletter No. 33   September 2016
What the 2016 Elections are All About - - Opportunity for All, Favoritism to None

We-the-People need a "new, New Deal" - - a promise to reduce the size and scope of an intrusive, ever-expanding, deficit-driven federal government. Using the benefit of 20/20 hindsight, FDR's "Old Deal" from the 1930's should never have been implemented. Unfortunately, those policies and programs represented the very first steps down the long and winding road towards Socialism. Our country desperately needs to change course, because the Old Deal and the "progressive" agenda is not working for America. Socialism, by its very nature, is contrary to the principles of limited government and individual rights that underlie the country's founding. Socialism might sound like a good idea (or might make you feel good) but history has shown that the detrimental effects of Socialism vastly outweigh any potential benefit of an ever-expanding federal government.

It is immoral to push $19.5 trillion of debt onto our children and grandchildren. This past month, the cumulative US debt amount surpassed the mark of $60,000 for every man, woman and child in America. Think about that statistic for just a moment, and then consider the fact that the Democratic Party's platform offers absolutely no ideas or solutions to the country's growing debt problem. Instead, it promises even more "free stuff" to favored segments of the country's citizens. This is truly immoral because our children and grandchildren have never had any input on the decisions that have been made to push this huge financial obligation onto them.

We need to eliminate deficit spending and begin re-paying the country's debt. We-the-People need to take our government back from the Washington cartel. Unfortunately, career politicians are not inclined to put forward solutions to this growing problem. They would rather try to continue to buy votes with other people's (our children's and grandchildren's) money. We need to implement Term Limits for the US Senate and US House of Representatives, so that the people who are running for Congress are free to fix this growing problem without being fearful of the possible effect on their long-term political career.

We need to stop talking about Tax Reform, and actually make fundamental (radical) changes to the tax code for personal income taxes. This includes linking Tax Reform to the related changes that need to be made for Social Security, Medicare / Healthcare taxes, and the country's poverty/welfare programs. We should not "tinker on the fringes", but we should use this opportunity to fundamentally transform (and shrink) the federal government.

We want the federal government to re-focus on its proper role - - the duties and responsibilities that are laid out in the US Constitution - - to protect the citizens' rights, protect the country as a whole, and manage our country's relationships with other countries around the world.

Thomas Paine in his pamphlet entitled "Common Sense" discussed the fundamental differences between government and civil society (families, religious institutions, charitable organizations, and other "communities"). The Progressive Agenda is simple and straight-forward - - government must continue to grow to become the most powerful force in society, and nothing should compete with the government's "experts" who will develop a program to solve any problem that could happen in a person's life.

Last month, we provided links to the 2016 platforms of the Republican and Democratic parties. Unfortunately, these are 66-page and 55-page documents. Although we encourage you to read the entire platforms of both parties, we realize that this is a significant investment of time. Therefore, we have prepared two new Conversation Pieces that are on our Foundation's website that are excerpts from the two parties' platforms –

http://www.f2ppr.org/wp-content/uploads/2016/08/The-2016-Republican-Party-Platform.pdf and
http://www.f2ppr.org/wp-content/uploads/2016/08/The-2016-Democratic-Party-Platform.pdf

US Debt Clock - - August 1st - $59,899 per citizen / September 1st - $60,144

What the 2016 Elections are All About - - Part Two

Our Editorial Board believes that there is probably general agreement among our country's citizens that the federal government should promote a level playing field - - an equal opportunity for each citizen. America continues to be "The Land of Opportunity" – people have the opportunity to become whatever they want to be. But a key difference between the Right and the Left is in regards to understanding the fundamental difference between equality of opportunity and equality of outcomes (i.e., Socialism / Communism).

So, what does "Favoritism to None" mean? It simply means that the federal government should not advance any type of policy that benefits any particular segment of the country's citizens. There should not be any "crony capitalism". There should not be any special tax breaks given to any special interest group. There should not be any policies that attempt to "socially engineer" the country's citizens.

The underlying meaning behind the "general welfare" clause in the US Constitution has been perverted by the Left. The general welfare of our country's citizens is simply in reference to the federal government's responsibility to ensure the general welfare of the country as a whole (i.e., national defense), and to protect each citizen's rights (the level playing field discussed above). It was never intended to be a requirement to provide cash welfare payments to individual citizens, or "free" college, or subsidized healthcare, etc. As we have noted in earlier newsletters, there appears to be no limit to the Progressive agenda. The Left believes the US Constitution is a "living document" that should be interpreted to justify any program or policy that the Left would like to implement. Any program for any special interest group can be justified under the Left's definition of the general welfare clause, and there should not be any limitations placed on the federal government. The Left rejects the concept of "Favoritism to None".

The federal government also distorts the marketplace. All you need to do is look at the rising cost of education and healthcare to see the detrimental effects of the federal government's involvement and dollars. The federal government needs to remove itself from any commercial activity and minimize its role in the economy. The time has come to privatize the US Postal Service. (Contrary

to the Democratic Party's platform, the post office is not a "national treasure" –
it loses $5 billion a year). We also need to end the federal government's role in
Fannie Mae and Freddie Mac, and privatize those institutions. Much has
already been written about the federal government's role in creating the
housing bubble, along with the resulting credit market collapse during 2008.

Social Security and Medicare are unsustainable as currently constituted. Our
elected officials need to stop avoiding this reality, and begin addressing the
financial challenges that are facing these programs caused by the ongoing
changes in the country's demographics and the ongoing decrease in the
number of workers per retiree. Having said that.... Our country needs to
honor its commitments to current retirees. We also need to create a transition
plan for people over the age of 55 who are approaching retirement. Everyone
who has paid money into Social Security should get their money back (with
interest). But, going forward, no one should ever get more than that amount,
because anything above that amount represents theft from future generations.
We need to transform Social Security into a means-tested welfare benefit that
would be available to any retired citizen who needs such financial assistance.

Healthcare is not a "right" any more than food or housing is a right. Providing
for healthcare costs is a Personal Responsibility. We need to repeal Obamacare
and remove the federal government from the management of the country's
healthcare system. But we also need to move towards a new healthcare
system for all of the country's citizens – a system that doesn't show favoritism
towards employees versus the self-employed, or for healthy people versus
people with pre-existing conditions. Our Editorial Board recognizes that there
is an oversight role the government needs to perform in regards to the
healthcare ikndustry, but the country's healthcare system needs to remain
firmly within the private sector (the doctors and nurses, their patients,
hospitals, and healthcare insurance companies). This private market-based
healthcare system should continue to cover the vast majority of the country's
citizens (as was the case prior to Obamacare). We then need to implement a
second-tier "public" healthcare option (by transforming Medicaid) to cover
those citizens who cannot afford to (or who choose not to) participate in the
private healthcare marketplace. And each citizen needs to pay into this
"public" healthcare pool via payroll tax withholdings for medical care.

The federal government's welfare / poverty programs have been an absolute, abject failure. This result was inevitable, because this is not a proper role of the federal government - - it is a role of civil society. We need to get the federal government out of the welfare business by changing the federal income tax code to enable citizens to direct a portion of their federal tax obligations directly to those organizations that they wish to support, rather than have those funds coercively paid to the Washington cartel.

We recognize that the federal government has a valid regulatory oversight role that needs to be performed in any situation where "protecting the country as a whole" is involved. But we need to shrink the size of the federal bureaucracy (the administrative state). Once the US Senate and House of Representatives have determined (legislated) a particular regulation, the actual execution of a regulatory oversight role needs to be taken out of the federal bureaucracy, and be performed at the state and / or local level (financed by federal block grants, if necessary). We want a federal government so small you can barely see it.

We need to rebuild the US military after seven years of neglect, and we need to re-establish and strengthen our country's relationships with our allies. The federal government needs to change its focus away from internal domestic "social engineering" issues, and have our federal government re-focus on its role of being the world's leader. We agree that America should not be the world's policeman, but we can no longer afford to "lead from behind."

The Left will try to keep our government focused on their internal domestic "social engineering" agenda. We need to have our federal government re-focus its attention on its duties laid out in the Constitution.

US Debt Clock - - September 1st - $60,144 per citizen / October 1st - $60,208

Newsletter No. 35   November 2016
What the 2016 Elections Should Be All About

Our country's (long and painful) 2016 political season will conclude with the general election on Tuesday, November 8th. Our Editorial Board encourages every registered voter to go to the polls and vote your conscience as you cast your votes for the various federal, state and local candidates, based on your assessment of each candidate's "agenda" and platform, and whether they have earned your trust.

If you would like additional perspective as you sort through the issues, we recommend that you visit a non-partisan website (www.isidewith.com) and complete a 10-minute survey, which focuses on the issues (rather than the "personality" of a candidate). It is a wide-ranging survey with questions about social issues, the Constitution, the economy, education, the environment, healthcare, immigration, and other domestic and foreign policy issues. The response buttons are not simply just "yes" or "no" replies - - the survey allows you to customize your response, or you can submit your own stance on the issue. The survey is also a good way to figure out what is important to you in this election, as it allows you to "weight" the importance of the issue. The summary of the survey's results can be enlightening, so it's worth checking out.

Since the beginning of this year's election cycle, our Editorial Board has attempted to keep the focus on the principles of the two major political parties. As we have noted earlier, the full text of the two parties' platforms are available on the internet, and we are again providing the following links to two Conversation Pieces on our Foundation's website that contain excerpts from the two parties' platforms –

http://www.f2ppr.org/wp-content/uploads/2016/08/The-2016-Republican-Party-Platform.pdf
and
http://www.f2ppr.org/wp-content/uploads/2016/08/The-2016-Democratic-Party-Platform.pdf

The 2016 elections represent an opportunity to choose between a smaller, better-focused, limited government, versus an ever-expanding, deficit-driven, more intrusive federal government.

Our Editorial Board agrees with the title of Hillary Clinton's 1996 book – It Takes a Village (To Raise a Child). However, we strongly disagree with the Left's "progressive" agenda. The Left's solution to every issue is the federal government (its "experts", its multitude of federal programs, and its attempts to funnel money and influence to its favored special interest groups).

Our Editorial Board believes that the best kind of village to raise a self-reliant, personally responsible child is civil society - - a strong family unit headed by a mother and a father, supported by other family members (aunts and uncles and grandparents), and backed up by Not-for-Profit charities, religious institutions, excellent (rather than poor) "chosen" schools, and other local "communities". The worst kind of village is one headed up by "Big Brother", who is distant, out of touch, intrusive and coercive.

We encourage you to re-read the Seven Inevitable Results that arise from Big Government, which were listed in our August newsletter, and keep in mind the Tenth Amendment – *The powers not delegated to the United States by the Constitution, nor prohibited by it to the States, are reserved to the States respectively, or to the people.*

The choice is ours to make on November 8th.

US Debt Clock - - October 1st - $60,208 per citizen / November 1st - $60,976

Newsletter No. 36   December 2016
And Now the Difficult Work Begins

On November 8th, the American electorate declared "It is time to drain the swamp". Now that the elections are behind us, in the words of President-elect Trump, "… it is time for America to bind the wounds of division… and for us to come together as one united people."

Our Editorial Board believes that three main themes played out during the November elections. First and foremost, our country's citizens made a definitive statement that a top priority is to eliminate corruption and cronyism in our nation's capital. It was time to bring in an outsider, because in the eyes of many, the Washington cartel's career politicians had established an elite political class that is at odds with our country's "regular" citizens, who said "Enough is enough". One of the most important planks in President-elect Trump's "Contract With the American Voter" is a pledge to move forward with a Constitutional Amendment to impose term limits on all members of Congress. By passing and implementing such an amendment, our elected representatives will be free to make decisions that are the right ones for our country as a whole, rather than worry about how an extremely difficult decision might affect their long-term political career.

The election was also an initial step in the right direction of restoring the Founders' concept of Limited Government. We need to have our elected officials respect the Constitution they are sworn to preserve, protect and defend. Over the past eight years, there has been a growing sense that our citizens' rights were slowly being dwindled away. There was also a sense that maybe the government's "experts" weren't always right. Maybe we shouldn't have been trying to "fundamentally transform" the country or "socially engineer" the country's citizens, or show favoritism to this or that special interest group. Maybe the country's Commander in Chief shouldn't have been legislating using a phone and a pen. Maybe the Supreme Court shouldn't have been legislating either. Maybe the executive branch should have been enforcing the laws that are on the books, rather than picking and choosing which laws should be enforced. Maybe we were being taxed too much and weren't seeing an adequate return on our investment in the federal government and its many new programs and regulations. Maybe we didn't want to pay for "free" college for everyone. Maybe the federal government was just getting too big, intrusive, and out of touch.

And one of the most important outcomes of the election is that the long and steady march of the Left's "progressive" agenda has been momentarily halted. Unfortunately, the Left's agenda remains intact. All you need to do is re-read the excerpts of The 2016 Democratic Party Platform (on our Foundation's website) for a listing of the Left's priorities. One of the most alarming aspects of the 2016 election cycle was the emergence of the "Democratic Socialism" ideology advocated by Senator Bernie Sanders. Keep in mind that the "progressive" agenda dates back to early 1900's. It has had its many (failed) successes over the years, starting with the various Socialism programs put forward by FDR. The size of the federal government then took another giant leap forward during the 1960's with LBJ's "Great Society" programs. And most recently, Bernie Sanders and Hillary Clinton attempted to move our country further to the Left. Although Senator Sanders was successful in moving the Democratic Party further to the Left, We-the-People were successful in blocking the further advance of Socialism in America.

Having said all that…. The bulk of the hard work still remains. We need to have our federal government re-focus on its core responsibilities that are laid out in the US Constitution, and we need to fundamentally transform (and shrink) the federal government, and follow the wisdom of the Tenth Amendment in the Bill of Rights – *The powers not delegated to the United States by the Constitution, nor prohibited by it to the States, are reserved to the States respectively, or to the people.* Entitlement programs need to be reformed. We need to stop stealing from our children and grandkids. We need to eliminate deficit spending and start re-paying the country's cumulative debt. Obamacare needs to be repealed and replaced. We need to get the federal government out of the welfare business, and instead support Not-for-Profit organizations (The People's solutions) that will be much more effective in eliminating poverty in America. We need to re-affirm the concepts of self-reliance and Personal Responsibility, and that All Lives Matter. And our federal government needs to re-focus its efforts on advancing the following agenda – Opportunity for All, Favoritism to None.

Newsletter No. 37   January 2017
Personal Responsibility – Part One

On our website, we have a Conversation Piece entitled *"Why Mitt Romney's Comments About the 47% Were Not Correct"*. Please note that we do not disagree with the fact / statistic cited by Mr. Romney - - 47% of our country's citizens do not pay federal income taxes. However, we do take exception to the idea that we live in a country where 47% of our fellow citizens feel that they are "victims". We continue to believe that the vast majority of Americans agree we live in a truly exceptional country - a land of opportunity.

We also take exception to the implication that because the 47% do not pay federal income taxes, these citizens are somehow deadbeats. The truth is that virtually every person who participates in our country's economy (as an employee, or as a self-employed person) pays taxes to the federal government on the income that they earn. However, it is unfortunate that these tax payers are forced to redistribute a portion of their income to other recipients via Social Security and Medicare payroll taxes. And it is unfortunate that even with all of these payroll taxes and employer contributions, the deficits for these two "Democratic Socialism" programs contributed approximately $500 billion to the total $587 billion deficit last year.

And it's unfortunate that when you include Medicaid, welfare programs, and interest on the country's debt, the total of this "mandatory" spending now represents about 70% of the nearly $4 trillion the federal government spends each year. And this leaves just a fraction of the federal government's tax revenues available for national defense and the other responsibilities of the government listed in the Constitution.

So, how have we allowed our federal government to get us into this predicament? As Ben Franklin warned, *"When the people find that they can vote themselves money, that will herald the end of the republic."* Mr. Romney's solution to these problems (and the purpose of our Foundation) is to promote the concept of taking Personal Responsibility for your own life. Unfortunately, the Democratic Socialists would tend to disagree.

Many of us are familiar with one of Aesop's Fables about the (irresponsible) Grasshopper and the responsible, industrious Ant. Unfortunately, our federal government (via its many "non-Constitutional" social welfare programs) has fostered a sense of entitlement among a large portion of our country's citizens. But nowhere in the Constitution does it state that the federal government has a responsibility to provide for the essentials of everyday life (or a cash "pension" during your retirement years).

US Debt Clock - - December 1st - $61,262 per citizen / January 1st - $61,326

Newsletter No. 38   February 2017
Personal Responsibility – Part Two

In the document on our Foundation's website entitled The 2020 Initiative, we recommend that changes be made to the federal income tax code for personal income taxes, whereby individuals who make charitable contributions would receive a credit against their federal income tax obligation (rather than merely get an itemized deduction against their taxable income, which marginally reduces the amount of taxes they pay to the IRS). This will allow the taxpayer to self-direct a portion of their tax obligation to the organizations of their choice, and take these funds out of the hands of the federal government.

The primary reason for this recommendation is to reduce the size and scope of the federal government. As we have noted on our website, Article 1 Section 8 of the Constitution lists the very important (and very limited) responsibilities of the federal government. Unfortunately, over the course of the past century, our federal government has lost its focus in regards to its core responsibilities and has introduced innumerable "non-Constitutional" programs that attempt to either socially engineer the country's citizens or "solve" a person's problems (which the government will never be able to accomplish). And unfortunately, many of these "progressive" programs have created significant negative unintended consequences.

Some of the worst unintended consequences include creating a sense of entitlement among a large portion of our country's citizens, which has led to increasing amounts of taxes and skyrocketing unsustainable federal debt that is being pushed onto future generations. But one of the worst consequences has been creating a sense of dependency on the federal government (for food, housing, medical care, "free" education, etc., etc.) at the expense of encouraging individuals to assume Personal Responsibility for their own needs and wants.

And another unintended consequence is the long history of economic distortions that these programs have caused within the marketplace. Federal money has been the source of "much-higher-than-inflation" increases in the cost of education and healthcare. Federal money and innumerable federal housing programs have also served to distort the housing market and contributed to the housing bubble that led to the Great Recession. Once the federal government has been transformed (whereby it only receives enough funds to carry out its very important, limited responsibilities) it should no longer attempt to manage any other activity beyond its stated responsibilities (please refer to the Tenth Amendment), and the negative consequences listed above will begin to subside.

The other primary reason for these recommended changes is to shift funds from the federal government and redirect those funds to "civil society", which consists of a variety of effective and innovative Not-for-Profit charitable organizations. Given the choice between continuing to send their money to the Washington cartel versus a favored charity, people will send their money directly to those organizations they want to support. Another benefit is that these charities will need to compete for these contributions, which will encourage them to operate more efficiently and show more effective outcomes, or bear the consequence of a decrease in the funds they receive from the public. These free market principles are applicable to each of the types of operations mentioned above, including Education, which is the topic of next month's newsletter.

US Debt Clock - - January 1st - $61,326 per citizen / February 1st - $61,547

Newsletter No. 39   March 2017
Personal Responsibility – Education

In last month's newsletter, we talked about some of the unintended consequences that arise when the federal government attempts to fulfill a role that is not listed in the Constitution. This month's newsletter deals with the question of what role the federal government should play in regards to Education. Many of us are familiar with the following quote, which is oftentimes attributed to the 12th century rabbi Moses ben Maimon - - *Give a man a fish and you feed him for a day. Teach a man to fish and you feed him for a lifetime.*

We don't think that anyone would dispute the fact that one of the most important factors that helps to determine a person's success in life is a good education. Most of us would agree that the primary initial responsibility for an individual's education resides with his/her parents. But ultimately, the responsibility for daily, ongoing, lifetime education resides solely with the individual. Access to the best schools in the world and/or massive amounts of federal government money will not change the fact that education is a Personal Responsibility.

So, what is the proper role for the federal government? Interestingly, the issue / topic of education is nowhere to be found in the US Constitution. But having said that, our Editorial Board believes the federal government's initial foray into the realm of public education in 1867 was probably appropriate. The original Office of Education was a minor bureau within the Department of the Interior, and was created to collect information on schools and teaching that would help the States establish effective school systems. We believe that this approach was properly aligned with the Constitution's intent to promote the General Welfare (of the country as a whole). Unfortunately (similar to other examples of federal government over-reach) supporters of the progressive agenda deemed that this level of involvement was not adequate and the federal government should help "manage" education, rather than merely serve as a conduit of "best practices" information to the States and to local schools.

Ultimately, President Jimmy Carter, with the backing of the National Education Association, was successful in establishing a cabinet level Department of Education in 1979. What has followed since then is not surprising, but is truly troubling. The first budget for the Department provided for 3,000 federal government employees and an annual budget of $12 billion. In President Obama's final budget for fiscal 2017, he proposed a Department budget for 5,000 federal employees and a budget of $69 billion. In addition, the 2017 budget also proposed $140 billion of new "mandatory" spending over the upcoming 10-year period, over and above the annual "discretionary" budget.

But the biggest disappointment is that the measurable results of our country's education system has gone in the opposite direction. Since the 1960s and the LBJ era, our country's education standing in the world has continued to fall. We have gone from a country that was able to put a man on the moon, to one where our country currently ranks in the middle of the pack (or worse).

So, what went wrong? It's obviously not due to a lack of money. The Organization for Economic Cooperation and Development (OECD) is an organization of 34 countries whose purpose is to promote trade and economic growth. In an OECD study, it was noted that the United States spent $11,700 per full-time-equivalent student on elementary/high school education, which was 31 percent higher than the OECD average. At the postsecondary level, the US spent $26,600 per FTE student, which was 79 percent higher than the OECD average.

A similar study by the USC Rossier School of Education compared our country's education spending and performance versus eleven other countries. Our country is the clear leader in annual spending, but ranks 9th in Science performance and 10th in Math.

A more comprehensive study, the Third International Mathematics and Science Study, showed similar dismal results. At the 4ᵗʰ Grade Level, among 26 countries, the US ranked 12ᵗʰ in Math and 3ʳᵈ in Science. However, at the 8ᵗʰ Grade Level, among 41 countries, the US rankings slipped to 28ᵗʰ in Math and 17ᵗʰ in Science. And continuing the trend, by the end of high school, among 21 countries in the study, the US ranked 19ᵗʰ in Math and 16ᵗʰ in Science.

Next month – What can we do about it?

US Debt Clock - - February 1st - $61,547 per citizen / March 1st - $61,557

Newsletter No. 40   April 2017
Education – Part Two

In last month's newsletter, we began a discussion about the unintended consequences of the federal government's involvement in Education - - massive increases in spending, coupled with declining results. These unintended results are occurring at both the elementary / high school level and the post-secondary level. Although the problem of declining results is similar, the discussion of the various issues and how best to move forward need to be addressed separately.

Elementary / high school education is a purely local issue. The students, the parents, and the teachers are all local. In most regards (other than questions about finances and funding) K-12 education isn't even a state-level issue. Our Editorial Board believes that the federal government has virtually no role to play in local education issues. As we noted last month, the federal government's initial foray into the realm of public education was probably OK, because it was limited to collecting and disseminating "best practices" information to the States. Unfortunately, starting with the Head Start program in 1965, and followed by innumerable programs since then, the federal government began increasing its influence at the local level by providing funds to local school districts to advance these federal programs. By "purchasing" this influence, local schools are, in effect, held hostage by these federal dollars.

The federal government should no longer attempt to micromanage the delivery of K-12 education. Unfortunately, for many decades, progressive theories and the resulting federal programs have served to undermine traditional K-12 education, and education bureaucrats have taken control away from the local community. Parents, local school boards, and the teachers in the classrooms, need to come together to reverse this trend and put student-focused innovation ahead of top-down regulation. The answer to improving results at your local school is parental involvement and local control. We also need to re-direct moneys away from the federal government, and have it flow directly to Parent-Teacher Associations and other local nonprofit organizations that have been established to support local education. As we recommend in The 2020 Initiative, this can be accomplished by making changes to the federal income tax code, whereby taxpayers would receive a direct tax credit (rather than a deduction against income) for contributions made to organizations that have been established to support local education.

Our Editorial Board has a great deal of respect and appreciation for public school teachers, who play a vital role in the development of young adults. Unfortunately, we cannot say the same thing about the various teachers' unions, who appear to be solely focused on the wants of the union, rather than the needs of our country's students. Not surprisingly, teachers' unions are passionate opponents of school choice, charter schools and vouchers.

We would like nothing more than to have all of our public schools succeed and return to the high levels of quality outcomes that were achieved in the past. But if a particular school is failing its mission, we support a parent's right to enroll their child in a high-quality alternative. Ultimately, it is a matter of parental involvement to decide the best alternative for their child. School choice simply means having the freedom to choose between the local public school, a charter school, a private school, homeschooling, or some other alternative. We must be able to provide students in failing schools the opportunity to find a better alternative. School vouchers should be available to any student who resides in a district that is deemed to be failing.

There is also a growing sense that our public schools have been "dumbed down", and children who attend failing schools are no longer being adequately educated in the skills that will enable them to be productive individuals once they graduate from high school. Our public schools need to re-focus on teaching the fundamentals of reading, writing, arithmetic, and science. Unfortunately, when a school loses its focus on these basic skills, and begins to devote time to teaching a "politically correct curriculum", it steals time away from more important subjects, such as history and the US Constitution.

-    -   -   -   -

We close this month's newsletter with the following news update (because this didn't get a lot of press coverage this past month). On March 16th, the country's debt limit was reset to reflect the additional borrowings that have occurred since the debt limit was suspended in November 2015. We have now re-entered that phase whereby the Treasury Department must now manage our country's debt through "extraordinary measures". The Congressional

Budget Office projects that if the new debt limit remains unchanged, those measures will probably be exhausted (and the Treasury will run out of cash) sometime in the fall of 2017. The following is a link to a concise 4-page report from the CBO about what this all means –

https://www.cbo.gov/publication/52465

US Debt Clock - - March 1st - $61,557 per citizen / April 1st - $61,149

Do not get overly excited or overjoyed by this momentary decrease. Our country's long term financial problems have not yet been fixed.

Newsletter No. 41   **May 2017**
Education – Part Three

As we discussed in last month's newsletter, our biggest complaint about the federal government's over-reach into the realm of local K-12 education has been the abysmal return on the massive increase in federal spending, coupled with the simultaneous decrease in measurable results. We attribute most of this decline to the federal government's top-down regulations and its attempts to enforce a politically correct curriculum, instead of letting parents, the local community, and their schools focus on the fundamentals of education that need to be provided to elementary and high school students. To paraphrase Carly Fiorina's presidential campaign slogan, "We need to take our local schools back from the federal government."

Having said that…. The federal government's detrimental effects on post-secondary education has been even worse. As we have noted elsewhere on our website, one of the worst unintended consequences of federal government spending is the price distortion it causes in the marketplace. We see this effect in healthcare, in housing, and in the cost of post-secondary education.

The crisis in outstanding student loan debt was created by the federal government, and the magnitude of this problem has increased ever since the government first expanded its role under President Bill Clinton in 1993. Since then, college costs have risen by 190 percent, far surpassing the overall rate of inflation. As the federal government took over student lending, the conditions for getting a loan were eased and were no longer linked to financial need. This has enabled all colleges (public and private) to raise tuition at will, knowing that students can get loans to cover the rising costs.

The student loan crisis has ballooned since 2003, when outstanding student loans totaled $240 billion. Total student loan debt now stands at $1.4 trillion (more than 85% guaranteed by the government), which is more than the amount of outstanding vehicle loans and credit card obligations, and is second only to mortgages. (And we all witnessed the detrimental effects of the federal government's role in the housing industry).

The progressive movement's solution is to make a public college education "free". But what will that do to the competition between public versus private colleges? (OK, that was a rhetorical question). The other solution is to "forgive" outstanding loan balances (in other words, make past student loans "free"). But is that fair to those responsible individuals who have actually paid off their student loans?

A first step towards solving the student loan problem is to eliminate all federal government student loan programs, and return the issuance of student loans to the private sector. Only then will the marketplace for post-secondary education begin to hold tuition costs in check. We also need to re-think the cost versus benefit of a college education. Is a four-year college degree really the right answer for every student? There are many different trades / occupations that do not require a degree, and there are labor shortages for these positions. (We plan to address the cost/benefit analysis of welfare versus work in a later newsletter).

The skills gap in our country is substantial, which is partly due to the poor results of the K-12 education system. In a recent survey, 45% of small business owners reported that they were unable to find qualified job applicants, including construction workers, truck drivers, automotive technicians, etc. Skills-training partnerships between business leaders and local high schools, colleges and community-based organizations, along with apprenticeships and internships, would help job candidates obtain the necessary skills.

Technology changes and other evolutions within the business world will continue to create a situation where workers need to be trained and retrained throughout their careers. Post-secondary education now represents a lifetime commitment to additional ongoing training. Public-private partnerships (funded by civil society) will be critical to improving the prosperity of all American workers.

One other issue of note - - Our Editorial Board's biggest complaint about the liberal / progressive movement's assault on our post-secondary education system can be summed up by this quote from Vladimir Lenin – *Give me four years to teach the children and the seed I have sown will never be uprooted.* Many of us recall the Free Speech Movement during the mid-1960s on the campus of the University of California, Berkeley. Now, Berkeley's administration is advocating "Free Speech Zones", which is an "Orwellian" term used to describe an approach whereby certain public speakers are literally put out of sight in a safe zone, in order to protect the rest of the student population from potentially "politically incorrect" points of view. My, oh my, how the world has "progressed" over the past several decades.

US Debt Clock - - April 1st - $61,149 per citizen / May 1st - $61,220

Newsletter No. 42   June 2017
Healthcare Re-Visited

On our website, we have an October 2013 Conversation Piece entitled *Medicare and Universal Health Care Coverage*. One of the main planks of Donald Trump's presidential campaign was to repeal and replace the (Un)Affordable Care Act (aka Obamacare), which has proven to be a disastrous over-reach by the federal government into our country's healthcare system. Unfortunately, the House of Representatives bundled the repeal initiative with the replacement initiative (which should have been dealt with separately in a second step). Fortunately, a second, better version of the American Health Care Act was passed by the House, and is now in the process of being re-written by the Senate. Hopefully, the final version of this legislation will serve to eliminate the fundamental flaws of Obamacare.

On our website, we have posted a new Conversation Piece entitled *Healthcare Re-Visited* –

http://www.f2ppr.org/wp-content/uploads/2017/06/Healthcare-ReVisited.pdf

In this posting, we distinguish between two separate issues - - "healthcare" (which is a Personal Responsibility) and acquiring a health insurance policy (which is also a Personal Responsibility). Unfortunately, the Socialists of the Left continue to link these two issues together in their ongoing attempts to further expand the size and scope of the federal government. By proclaiming that healthcare is a "right", they attempt to make the case that people should no longer be responsible for their own healthcare, because healthcare should be administered by the federal government.

We also provide a little history on employer group health insurance plans, and we discuss the similarities and difference between health insurance and other types of insurance, like auto insurance. We also put forward our recommendations on how each of our country's citizens can acquire a health insurance policy that meets their own individual needs, and we address the issues regarding what can be done on behalf of those citizens who need financial assistance to acquire a health insurance policy.

US Debt Clock - - May 1st - $61,220 per citizen / June 1st - $61,297

Newsletter No. 43   July 2017
Personal Responsibility - Food and Housing

In our newsletters the past few months, we have tried to promote the concept that education and healthcare are Personal Responsibilities. However, the Socialists of the Left want to change our citizens' mindset by re-labeling these aspects of daily life as being new "rights" that give rise to new "entitlements". This is simply part of the Left's "progressive" agenda to increase the size and scope of the federal government. Unfortunately, if the Socialists are successful in regards to education and healthcare, the same thinking can then be applied to the concept of an "entitlement" to food and housing. And after that.... Who knows?

Compassionate conservatives recognize the fact that food and housing are "needs". Conservatives agree that there is no reason why a citizen in our country of plenty should go hungry or homeless, and also acknowledge that some of our country's citizens require assistance to have their needs met. Where Conservatives and Socialists disagree is in regards to the methods to make this happen. The Socialists believe in the coercive powers of the federal government, which they try to sell to the public as being "federal government benevolence". The federal government was not set up to be benevolent. (See Thomas Paine's *Common Sense* comments about government). Conservatives believe in Personal Responsibility and families and Not-for-Profit charities - this is a far better method of taking care of our citizens' needs, rather than relying on yet another inefficient, counter-productive government program.

Our Editorial Board believes that the waste, inefficiency, and corruption of the federal government prevents it from effectively accomplishing any of its stated welfare goals. In *The 2020 Initiative*, our Editorial Board proposes a fundamental change to the US tax code for personal income taxes, whereby a charitable contribution to a Not-for-Profit charity will result in a tax credit against an individual's / family's federal income tax obligation that would otherwise be paid into the swamp. The federal government needs to be starved of these funds, so that it no longer intrudes into the marketplace for education, healthcare, food, housing, or any other aspect of daily life. Its focus should be on the federal government's responsibilities that are specifically listed in the US Constitution.

In *The 2020 Initiative*, we recommend that four independent national Not-for-and education. The sole purpose of these national charities would be to collect funds from citizens, and then (based on stringent, objective criteria that quantifies each state's needs) disburse that charity's funds to the applicable state-level charitable organization in each state.

As we will discuss in our upcoming Conversation Piece on *Welfare Reform Re-Visited*, the real solution to the issue of poverty is to help those less fortunate become "unpoor". The Socialists' "default solution" to any issue is to have the federal government simply provide cash to people who need assistance. But this approach only serves to increase the sense of entitlement among our country's citizens, and increases the recipient's dependency on the federal government, while only marginally and temporarily helping the recipient become "somewhat less poor". The better solution is to provide financial support to local community-based social services agencies (local job training programs, food banks, habitat for humanity groups, public health clinics, etc.) so that civil society can help citizens assume Personal Responsibility for their own lives, lift themselves out of poverty, and become unpoor.

US Debt Clock - - June 1st - $61,297 per citizen / July 1st - $61,368

Newsletter No. 44   August 2017
Personal Responsibility – Your Savings for Your Retirement Years

It has been a few months since we last discussed Social Security, so our Editorial Board thought that this would be a good month to re-visit this issue. We do this for three reasons.

Our elected representatives will soon be returning to Washington DC from their August break, to vote on increasing the federal government's so-called "debt limit" (which has become a farce that is increasingly irrelevant and meaningless).

They will also be trying to put the finishing touches on our federal government's fiscal 2018 budget for the year that begins on October 1st. All of the projections show that this budget will not "balance", and therefore over the course of the upcoming year, there will continue to be an increase in the total debt of the federal government.

But most importantly, we want to point out the fact that very few of our elected representatives are brave enough to address the issue of entitlement reform. They do not want to come forward with a solution to this problem, because they are worried about what effect this would have on their next re-election. Currently, approximately 70% of the federal government's spending is on automatic pilot for "mandatory" spending.... Mandatory?? How did we ever get into this mess? The answer is very simple - - Many years ago "progressive" politicians (including FDR) decided that retirement funds should become the responsibility of the federal government (instead of being a Personal Responsibility). And then in the 1960s, another career politician (LBJ) along with other Socialists of the Left added Medicare, Medicaid and various welfare programs to the list.

In *The 2020 Initiative*, our Editorial Board puts forward our thoughts on how Social Security can be transformed over a multi-year transition period into a means-tested welfare benefit. As we have noted previously, there is no money in the Social Security "Trust" (which is another misleading federal government charade). But even though we believe it is immoral for the federal government to continue to steal funds from future generations to make Social Security payments to other people, we are "somewhat OK" with the idea of a means-tested welfare benefit for an elderly retired citizen who is in need of financial assistance. We acknowledge the possibility that due to an individual's facts and circumstances, they might not have been able to personally save enough funds that would have allowed them to cover their own needs over the course of their retirement years. In that type of situation, our first choice would normally be to have civil society (families, supported by Not-for-Profit charities and other local social services agencies) provide this kind of assistance to such an individual, but maybe it's OK for the federal government to provide for such a means-tested welfare benefit.

Having said that... Our country's citizens need to begin to acknowledge that even this kind of means-tested welfare benefit is not a proper role of the federal government. And unfortunately, the payments that are currently being made under this program do not make any sense - - the vast majority of these "unfunded pension benefits" are being paid to retirees who are probably already financially secure, and only minimal monthly amounts are being paid to retirees who probably need to receive a Social Security benefit (see the July 2015 letter to Senator Bernie Sanders on our Foundation's website).

In its current form, this government program is unsustainable. As the program's Trustees have reported for the past several years, "*Lawmakers should address the projected trust fund shortfalls in a timely way in order to phase in necessary changes gradually and give workers and beneficiaries time to adjust to them.*" Congress, are you listening? We are extremely disappointed that we hear this "standard" wording in the Trustees' report year after year after year. Maybe (soon?) our elected officials will finally take the steps that are needed to fundamentally transform this failing government program. Our proposed transition plan would not change any benefits to retirees who are currently receiving Social Security payments. It would also allow current workers to get their personal contributions back out of the Social Security program, plus interest. But after that, the federal government would no longer be able to coercively tax future generations for unfunded promises that were made in the past. Unless these fundamental changes occur (soon), it is going to be extremely difficult for future generations to save for their own retirement years.

US Debt Clock - - July 1st - $61,368 per citizen / August 1st - $61,344

Newsletter No. 45   September 2017
Welfare Reform Re-Visited

Fair warning to all readers who might have "Democratic Socialism" tendencies.... Continue reading at your own risk. On our website, we have added a new Conversation Piece entitled *Welfare Reform Re-Visited* -

http://www.f2ppr.org/wp-content/uploads/2017/09/Welfare-Reform-Revisited.pdf

In this Conversation Piece, we provide our thoughts on how to repeal and replace the federal government's counter-productive welfare programs. Our country needs to face a sobering fact - - our federal government has lost its "War on Poverty". History and events have proven that LBJ's Great Society welfare programs have been an abject failure. We have spent over $22 trillion on welfare programs since the 1960s, and the percentage of people who live in poverty has remained virtually unchanged.

The definition of insanity is doing the same thing over and over again, while expecting to achieve a different result. We need to fundamentally transform welfare (which is simply the delivery of goods and services to citizens who need assistance). With this Conversation Piece, our Editorial Board is launching our own war on the War on Poverty. The welfare programs sponsored by our federal government cannot solve the problem of poverty (contrary to how these programs have been "marketed" to the public in the past). Instead, these welfare programs have only served to foster a growing sense of entitlement among our country's citizens and have increased the level of dependency on the federal government.

Our Editorial Board's alternative is to promote the concept of Personal Responsibility, rather than Socialism. An individual who is in poverty should look to assistance from civil society for the solution to their problem(s), rather than a government program. History has proven without a doubt that the federal government's programs cannot accomplish the objective of reducing poverty.

LBJ's Great Society programs were a drastic over-reach by the federal government. The federal government was not established by the States to deliver welfare to individual citizens. It was set up to protect our country's citizens' lives and liberties, and our ability to pursue happiness. The General Welfare clause in the Constitution refers to policies and programs that promote the General Welfare of the country as a whole, and does not refer to providing welfare benefits to individual citizens.

Having said that… Compassionate citizens of all political persuasions recognize that some individuals are going to need some assistance during some period of time in their life. The poor have always lived among us, and this has been true going all the way back to pre-biblical times. As we noted in *The 2020 Initiative*, the real solution to the problem of poverty is to help the poor become "unpoor". However, one of the first steps that needs to happen is for each individual to develop a game plan to take Personal Responsibility for their own life. A sense of Personal Responsibility (instead of a sense of "vicitimization") combined with the assistance available from civil society (families, supported by local community groups, charities, and social service agencies) is the only means by which a person will become unpoor. For those on the Left who are brave enough, please launch the link to the Conversation Piece entitled *Welfare Reform Re-Visited*.

-    -   -   -   -

As many of us recall, on October 30, 2015, legislation was passed to suspend the federal government's debt limit to March 2017. Since then, the Treasury department has employed "extraordinary measures" to continue meeting federal obligations without issuing new debt, and the amount of debt has been stalled at approximately $19.97 trillion since July. However, these extraordinary measures will become depleted some time later this month. Unfortunately, the incremental costs that have been incurred for these extraordinary measures total approximately $2.5 billion. But this amount is "miniscule" when you consider the fact that the annual deficit for this year is going to be around $600 billion.

US Debt Clock - - August 1st - $61,344 per citizen / September 1st - $61,330

Newsletter No. 46   October 2017
Other Thoughts on Personal Responsibility

Just a short newsletter this month – we are providing the following link to another new Conversation Piece on our Foundation's website entitled *Other Thoughts on Personal Responsibility* –

http://www.f2ppr.org/wp-content/uploads/2017/10/Other-Thoughts-on-Personal-Responsibility.pdf

In addition to promoting the concept of personal responsibility, our Editorial Board also believes in the concepts of Opportunity for All and Favoritism to None. This is where the federal government's focus should be.

Unfortunately, the Left supports Big Government and intrusive regulations that diminish Opportunities for All. The Socialists of the Left condemn corporations (along with successful, wealthy individuals) as being the source of all evil in society. But here is a fundamental question -   - If corporations and other businesses are not the means by which our citizens receive goods and services, who is going to provide the jobs (and opportunities) that people need in order to have a meaningful purpose in life? Of course, the Socialists' default answer is "Big (more) Government". But history has shown that Socialism doesn't work - a government does not and cannot create wealth – it can only re-distribute wealth.

Having said that…. It is very true that a very significant problem exists - - Corruption occurs under "crony capitalism". However, this corruption is oftentimes due to collusion between career politicians and special interest groups, and this collusion violates the concept of "Favoritism to None."

The federal government was established to militarily defend the country as a whole, and to protect our citizen's rights. Period. (Please re-read the Tenth Amendment). When the federal government attempts to expand beyond this limited role, bad things begin to happen. Forrest Gump (and his mom) were fond of saying "Stupid is as stupid does". Unfortunately, the federal government is currently doing a lot of stupid things.

-    -   -   -   -

We close this month's newsletter with a sobering piece of news, which should come as no surprise to the members of our Foundation. Our federal government's finances are on an unsustainable path, and unfortunately this past month, our country passed a new threshold. The federal government's cumulative debt now stands in excess of $20 trillion (and continues to rise)….

Newsletter No. 47   **November 2017**
Other Musings

One year ago, our country's citizens decided that we do not want a bigger, more intrusive federal government. Unfortunately, the Socialists of the Left are not going to go away quietly. This month, we are providing a link to another new Conversation Piece on our Foundation's website entitled *Other Musings* –

http://www.f2ppr.org/wp-content/uploads/2017/10/Other-Musings.pdf

The federal government's cumulative debt amount continues to rise. The members of our Foundation need to stay engaged in this conversation with our elected officials, and need to continue to deliver the message that "enough is enough". Our elected officials need to either deliver a solution, or they will be voted out of office.

We close this month's newsletter with another one of our favorite Forrest Gump quotes. Whenever Forrest was finished articulating yet another self-evident truth, he would sum it all up by saying "That's all I have to say about that."

The Foundation to Promote Personal Responsibility

Our Editorial Board

The members of our Foundation's Editorial Board are a group of "average Joes", along with a few "average Jills". Several of us went to the same college and have a business background, rather than a political background. Collectively, we have extensive experience in the business world, and therefore, we tend to approach many of our country's issues from a "business and economics" perspective, rather than a "political" perspective. In our discussions, we focus on the state of the world - - what is good and right, and what problems need fixing. We debate the merits of various ideas, and discuss possible changes that could be implemented to keep our country strong, free and prosperous.

We do not always agree 100%, but each of the postings on our Foundation's website has been approved by a majority of our Editorial Board members. Some of our Conversation Pieces have gone through a number of re-writes over the years, and have evolved to where they are today, as we try to incorporate new wisdom, and new thoughts, ideas, and recommendations.

There is one thing upon which we all agree - - simply exercising our right to vote is not enough. We believe that our country's citizens need to become more knowledgeable about the functioning of our governmental units, and re-engage more directly in the political process. We are alarmed at the growing level of voter apathy. (At times, it seems like this might be one of objectives of the two political parties - - to further create a divide between We-the-People and the political "elites" in Washington DC). We need to encourage our fellow citizens to become more actively involved, so that our federal, state and local governments begin to live within their means (currently / now), and stop borrowing against future generations. If we can accomplish that feat, we still have a chance to successfully avert our country's looming debt crisis.

Our Editorial Board's objective is to facilitate a nation-wide conversation about the breakdown of fiscal responsibility in government. We welcome receiving feedback from our Foundation's members, along with their thoughts, new ideas, and recommendations. We highlight current "news events" and share new ideas and recommendations in our monthly newsletter. We encourage you to become a member of our Foundation, Join the Conversation, and Promote Personal Responsibility.

Our primary author is Tim Beck, a semi-retired CPA, business consultant and financial analyst. Although he is not a "tax practitioner", he is knowledgeable about the US tax code for both businesses and personal income tax returns. The bottom line is that our Editorial Board is appalled at how our elected officials have increasingly used the tax code to violate the principle of Favoritism to None.